Preface

This book contains a revised version of my *Habilitationsschrift* which has been accepted by the economic department of Dortmund University in 1991. It consists mostly of unpublished material which has been presented during the last years at the universities of Cologne, Dortmund, Hagen, Mannheim, and Munich and at a meeting in Wiesbaden.

I am indebted to very many collegues for fruitful discussions. In particular, I want to thank Friedrich Breyer, Johannes Hoffmann, Heinz Holländer, Wolfgang Leininger, Bruno Schönfelder, Gerhard Schwödiauer, Hans-Werner Sinn, Klaus Spremann, and Jochen Weimann, but this list is surely incomplete. I am especially grateful, however, to Wolfram F. Richter and Niko Wolik who have continually accompanied the evolution of this work and to whom I owe many suggestions as well as corrections. The remaining errors, needless to say, are mine.

Cologne, September 1991   Stefan Homburg

Stefan Homburg

Efficient Economic Growth

Springer-Verlag
Berlin Heidelberg New York
London Paris Tokyo
Hong Kong Barcelona
Budapest

Professor Dr. STEFAN HOMBURG
Wirtschaftstheoretische Abteilung II
Universität Bonn
Adenauerallee 24-42
D-5300 Bonn 1, FRG

ISBN 3-540-54995-1 Springer-Verlag Berlin Heidelberg New York Tokyo
ISBN 0-387-54995-1 Springer-Verlag New York Berlin Heidelberg Tokyo

This work is subject to copyright. All rights are reserved, whether the whole or part of the material is concerned, specifically the rights of translation, reprinting, reuse of illustrations, recitation, broadcasting, reproduction on microfilms or in other ways, and storage in data banks. Duplication of this publication or parts thereof is only permitted under the provisions of the German Copyright Law of September 9, 1965, in its version of June 24, 1985, and a copyright fee must always be paid. Violations fall under the prosecution act of the German Copyright Law.

© Springer-Verlag Berlin · Heidelberg 1992
Printing in Germany

The use of registered names, trademarks, etc. in this publication does not imply, even in the absence of a specific statement, that such names are exempt from the relevant protective laws and regulations and therefore free for general use.

2142/7130-543210 - Printed on acid-free paper

Contents

Chapter 1. Introduction 1

Chapter 2. Dynamic Efficiency 3
   2.1 The Basic Model 3
   2.2 A General Theorem on Dynamic Efficiency 9
   2.3 Some Further Results 12
   2.4 Storable Consumer Goods 14
   2.5 The Failure of the First Basic Welfare Theorem 17
   2.6 A Stronger Condition 20
   2.7 A Remark on Necessary Conditions 21
   2.8 Conclusion 22

Chapter 3. Interest and Growth 25
   3.1 Commodity Own Rates of Interest 26
   3.2 The Asset-augmented Economy 28
   3.3 Interest, Growth, and Dynamic Efficiency 31
   3.4 Conclusion 33
   Appendix: The Cash Flow Criterion 34

Chapter 4. An Economy with Land 39
   4.1 A Characterization of Land 40
   4.2 Land as a Consumption Good 41
   4.3 Land as a Factor of Production 43
   4.4 The Land's Income Share 45
   4.5 Land and Dynamic Efficiency 46
   4.6 A Stronger Efficiency Result 48
   4.7 Conclusion 50

Chapter 5. Exhaustible Resources 53
   5.1 A Characterization of Exhaustible Resources 53
   5.2 Exhaustible Resources as Consumption Goods 55
   5.3 Exhaustible Resources as Factors of Production 56
   5.4 The Hotelling Rule 57
   5.5 Exhaustible Resources and Dynamic Efficiency 59
   5.6 Efficient Use of Exhaustible Resources 61
   5.7 Conclusion 64

Chapter 6. Examples and Applications 65
   6.1 Dynamic Efficiency in a Simple Growth Model 65
   6.2 A Simple Economy with Land 71
   6.3 Turgot's Theory of Fructification 78
   6.4 A Capital Reserve System without Capital 83
   6.5 Old Masters and Bubbles 88
   6.6 A Simple Economy with an Exhaustible Resource 92

References 97

Name Index 103

Subject Index 105

Chapter 1. Introduction

The present monograph deals with *Efficient Economic Growth*. This title has deliberately been chosen so as to distinguish the problem we want to analyze from the older concept of *Optimal Economic Growth*. Most contemporary writers, I think, do not believe in the existence of "an" optimal growth path if the term "optimal" is to bear any precise meaning. In a model of economic growth there generally exists a variety of *Pareto-optimal*, i.e. *efficient*, growth paths, but other paths may well be inefficient. And this is the main issue we want to investigate: How can efficient growth paths be characterized? And can we believe that growth in our actual market economies is efficient indeed?

These problems are not new, nor are the methods we use in order to analyze them. But the study tries to bring together two strands of growth theory. The first consists of rather primitive models of the one-sector type and concentrates heavily on *steady state growth*, which is both a special and an unrealistic assumption. The other strand, encompassing the microeconomic overlapping-generations literature, is much in the spirit of static general equilibrium theory à la Arrow-Debreu, yet at the same time sterile and certainly not in a position to answer the questions growth theorists habitually ask. In closing the gap between these two strands we gradually develop a unifying theory of economic growth which focuses on efficiency problems and reveals the common underlying structure of many issues encountered in this field. We also derive a plausible condition that ensures *dynamic efficiency* – the latter term being used as a short-hand for "Pareto-optimality in a dynamic model with an unbounded horizon".

The framework used throughout the text is a microeconomic overlapping-generations model with both consumption and production activities, with finitely lived agents, and without bequests. The reason for selecting precisely these assumptions is a strategic one: It is well-known that dynamic inefficiency does not occur in a model with infinitely lived agents and without bequests – the problem is specific to worlds where all agents have finite lifespans, such as the world we live in. And as Weil (1987) has shown, a bequest motive of the type proposed by Barro (1974), will *not* preclude dynamic inefficiency. Just the other way round, inefficiency will render operative bequests *impossible*. Therefore, the introduction of a Barro-type bequest motive would make the analysis notationally more complicated without changing the basic results (though different results may emerge in a setting with bequests and strategic behaviour, where the generations play against one another).

On the other hand, it seemed worthwhile to include production and to admit arbitrarily many types of agents and commodities per period. For notational convenience only, we also imposed a specific structure on the model in assuming that all agents live for two periods. This is not restrictive because, as Balasko, Cass and Shell (1980) have demonstrated so nicely, every two-period lifetime model can be interpreted as a n-period lifetime model by simply redefining indices – provided that the number of agents living in every period is arbitrary. In this sense, and because no special behavioural assumptions are employed, our framework can be thought of as a quite general model of economic growth.

The text is virtually divided into two parts, the first encompassing chapters 2 to 5, and the second consisting of chapter 6 only. The analysis in the first part is general, abstract, and there we try to give definitive answers to the questions we ask. The second part is special, vivid, and full of examples, and it does not contain any result which goes beyond the theorems of the first part. Experts in the field will presumably consider the second part as a collection of teaching examples whilst newcomers may want to start reading with chapter 6 which motivates the preceding analysis.

Chapter 2. Dynamic Efficiency

In the present chapter we first want to give a general characterization of dynamic efficiency by means of a microeconomic growth model which closely resembles the models known from static general equilibrium theory à la Arrow-Debreu. After having outlined the basic framework, we derive our main result and add some interpretations. Thereafter, a sequence of simpler conditions for dynamic efficiency will be given.

An essential feature of our approach is that we concentrate solely on dynamic efficiency during the entire chapter. All of our assumptions are made with a view to this aim. In particular, existence problems are not discussed, and our premises are obviously not sufficient to ensure existence of equilibrium. This course has been deliberately chosen for the following reason: Existence of equilibrium may be due to some assumptions or others — in any case one has to be more specific about the economy under consideration and thus has to restrict the scope of the analysis. We maintain that the issue of dynamic efficiency can be separated from related problems such as existence or determinacy of equilibrium and is only obscured when these are discussed at the same time.

2.1 The Basic Model

This section contains a description of our economy and all assumptions which are employed in the sequel. The model is relatively straightforward, but the notation used may appear a bit complicated because in overlapping-generations — as opposed to static — models every commodity and every agent must be specified by both a type and a time index. Our economy covers a finite number of commodities, households and firms per period. The total numbers, however, are infinite.

Among our notational conventions are: All *time* indices are *subscripts*. Thus x_t etc. denotes some commodity bundle in period t. All indices which refer to *agents* are *superscripts*. Thus x^a etc. denotes the commodity bundle of agent no. *a*. Consequently, x_t^a is used to denote the commodity bundle of agent a at time t. Indices which refer to a specific *commodity* are also *superscripts*. There can be no misunderstanding because such indices are rarely used. But if we want to designate commodity i of agent a at time t, we write $x_t^{a,i}$.

Commodities and prices: In every period $t \in \mathbb{N}$ there are $n \in \mathbb{N}$ different commodities, including consumption and capital goods as well as labour services. The quantities demanded by a household (or supplied by a firm) are denoted by positive numbers, and the quantities supplied by a household (or demanded by a firm) by negative numbers. $e_t = (e_t^1, e_t^2, ..., e_t^n)$ is the total *initial endowment* in period t; it is a point in $\mathbb{R}^n$. $e = (e_1, e_2, e_3, ...)$ is the sequence of total initial endowments, and e^i depicts the sequence of endowments of the i-th good. $p_t = (p_t^1, p_t^2, ..., p_t^n)$ is the price vector in period t; it is a point in $\mathbb{R}^n_{++}$. $p = (p_1, p_2, p_3, ...)$ is the sequence of price vectors. Price sequences are normalized by $p_1^1 = 1$. A price p_t^i therefore gives the *present value* of commodity i at time t in terms of commodity 1 at time 1.

Households: The household $h \in \mathbb{N}$ is a pair $(X^h, \succcurlyeq_h)$, consisting of a consumption-set $X^h \subset \mathbb{R}^{2n}$ and a preference ordering $\succcurlyeq_h$. $H_t \subset \mathbb{N}$ is the finite set of households born in period t. "Born" means: A household $h \in H_t$ chooses a point (x_t^h, x_{t+1}^h) in its consumption-set X^h, the index t referring to the period where consumption takes place. The choice is depicted by the vector $x^h = (x_t^h, x_{t+1}^h)$ which is sometimes written as a sequence $x^h = (0, 0, ..., x_t^h, x_{t+1}^h, 0, ...)$. There are also households born in period 0, for which we set $x_0^h = 0$. When referring to the i-th (i = 1...n) commodity in the bundle x_t^h, we write $x_t^{h,i}$.

Assumption 1: For every household $h \in H_t$,

the consumption-set X^h is convex;	(1.1)
the preference ordering $\succcurlyeq_h$ is convex;	(1.2)
no $x^h \in X^h$ is a local satiation point;	(1.3)
X^h is bounded from below by $u^h = (u_t^h, u_{t+1}^h) \in \mathbb{R}^{2n}$.	(1.4)

"Convexity" of preference orderings is understood to mean the following: If x^h and $\bar{x}^h$ are two elements of a household's consumption-set X^h such that x^h is strictly preferred to $\bar{x}^h$, then every convex combination

$t \cdot x^h + (1-t) \cdot \bar{x}^h$ will also be strictly preferred to $\bar{x}^h$, where $0 < t < 1$. Assumptions (1.1) to (1.3) are also employed by Debreu (1959) in his proof of the first basic welfare theorem whilst assumption (1.4) is usually made in existence proofs only.

By definition, the *commodity bundle* x^h contains consumption goods as well as labour services. It will be convenient to denote a household's *consumption* by

$$c^h := x^h - u^h \geq 0. \tag{1.5}$$

The components of u^h are zero for the goods demanded by the household and negative for the services supplied by the household. Thus c^h gives total consumption, including leisure. For instance, if $x_t^h = (5; -3)$ and $u_t^h = (0; -10)$, we have $c_t^h = (5; 7)$: The household consumes five units of the consumption good and 7 units of leisure.

Firms: The firm $f \in \mathbb{N}$ is characterized by a production-set $Y^f \subset \mathbb{R}^{2n}$. $F_t \subset \mathbb{N}$ is the finite set of firms founded in period t. "Founded" means: A firm $f \in F_t$ chooses a point (y_t^f, y_{t+1}^f) in its production-set Y^f, the index t referring to the period where production takes place. The choice is depicted by the vector $y^f = (y_t^f, y_{t+1}^f)$ which is sometimes written as a sequence $y^f = (0, 0, ..., y_t^f, y_{t+1}^f, 0,...)$. There are also firms founded in period 0, for which we set $y_0^f = 0$. When referring to the i-th commodity (i = 1...n) in the bundle y_t^f, we write $y_t^{f,i}$.

Assumption 2: Consider a firm $f \in F_t$ and define $s_t^f - k_t^f := y_t^f$ such that $k_t^f \geq 0$ and, for all i, either $s_t^{f,i} = 0$ or $k_t^{f,i} = 0$. We assume that for all firms and for all feasible production plans

$$\bar{y}^f, y^f \in Y^f \quad \text{implies} \quad (\bar{s}_t^f - k_t^f, y_{t+1}^f) \in Y^f. \tag{2}$$

This means that there is a clear-cut distinction between *static production*, represented by s_t^f, and *dynamic production*, represented by k_t^f (capital) and y_{t+1}^f: If some static production plan $\bar{s}_t^f$ is feasible, it remains feasible whatever are the values of k_t^f and y_{t+1}^f. And a feasible dynamic production plan $(-k_t^f, y_{t+1}^f)$ remains feasible irrespective of the values of $\bar{s}_t^f$. As both s_t^f and k_t^f can have a zero number of non-zero components, this is more a definition than an assumption.

The crucial assumption is $k_t^f \geq 0$ which demands that all present goods which technically influence – or are influenced by – future goods, are inputs: *It is impossible to produce present outputs using future inputs.* This premise is a fundamental property of any dynamic model; it reflects the one-directional nature of time. Consider two polar special cases of assumption 2 which are frequently encountered in the literature:

1) *Purely static production*: $k_t^f = 0$. Thus, if $(\bar{y}_t^f, \bar{y}_{t+1}^f)$ and (y_t^f, y_{t+1}^f) are feasible, $(\bar{y}_t^f, y_{t+1}^f)$ is also feasible, i.e. production in period t and production in period t+1 do not affect one another.

2) *Purely dynamic production*: $s_t^f = 0$ which implies $y_t^f = (0 - k_t^f) \leq 0$. In this case, all current goods are *inputs* so that younger firms can only invest but cannot produce instantaneously. Such an assumption is implicitly made, for instance, in Malinvaud (1953) or Cass (1972).

Allocations: Because households and firms live for two periods, all aggregate variables in period t result from the actions of only those agents who have come into existence in periods t-1 and t:

$$c_t := \sum_{H_{t-1}} c_t^h + \sum_{H_t} c_t^h, \qquad (3.1)$$

Total con-   = consumption of   +   consumption of
sumption   old households   of young households.

$$y_t := \sum_{F_{t-1}} y_t^f + \sum_{F_t} y_t^f, \qquad (3.2)$$

Total pro-   = production of   +   production of
duction   old firms   young firms.

$$x_t := \sum_{H_{t-1}} x_t^h + \sum_{H_t} x_t^h, \qquad (3.3)$$

$$k_t := \sum_{F_t} k_t^f. \qquad (3.4)$$

Concerning (3.4), observe that due to assumption 2, only the younger firms invest. The older firms can only use up the accumulated capital stock or sell capital goods to other agents (or engage in purely static production). This convention seems natural since, by investment, we imagine a process where future commodities are produced by means of current inputs.

An *allocation* is a pair $((x^h), (y^f))$ if $x^h \in X^h$ and $y^f \in Y^f$ for all households and firms. An allocation is *feasible* if $x_t - y_t = e_t$ for all t. By (x^h) we denote the sequence $(x^1, x^2, ...)$ which specifies each household's commodity bundle; and the sequence $(y^h) = (y^1, y^2, ...)$ specifies each firm's production plan. Hence, the pair $((x^h), (y^f))$ completely describes the distribution of commodities over all agents who are existing from the present to the indefinite future. The equation $x_t - y_t = e_t$ requires that the aggregate resource constraint be satisfied in each period $t = 1, 2, ...$ where x_t and y_t are defined by (3.3) and (3.2), respectively, and e_t is the initial endowment.

Definition (Competitive Equilibrium): An allocation $((\bar{x}^h), (\bar{y}^f))$ is a competitive equilibrium, supported by a price sequence p, if it is feasible, no household can make himself better off without spending more, and no firm can make higher profits:

$$\bar{x}_t - \bar{y}_t = e_t \qquad \text{for all t,} \qquad (4.1)$$

$$p \cdot x^h \leq p \cdot \bar{x}^h \text{ implies } x^h \leq_h \bar{x}^h \qquad \text{for all h and } x^h \in X^h, \qquad (4.2)$$

$$p \cdot y^f \leq p \cdot \bar{y}^f \qquad \text{for all f and } y^f \in Y^f. \qquad (4.3)$$

Equation (4.2) means that among the cheaper commodity bundles which are feasible for household h, none is preferred. This can be considered as an abstract budget constraint. We do not write down the budget constraints in a more specific form since nothing has been assumed about the distribution of initial endowments and profits among the households. Note that every equilibrium commodity bundle is signed with a bar (¯). The bar, however, is *not* used for equilibrium price sequences since all price sequences used are considered to support an equilibrium.

Definition (Pareto-optimum): A feasible allocation $((\bar{x}^h), (\bar{y}^f))$ is a Pareto-optimum if no household can be made better off without making another worse off, i.e. there exists no allocation $((x^h), (y^f))$ such that:

$$x_t - y_t = e_t \qquad \text{for all t,} \qquad (5.1)$$

$$x^h >_h \bar{x}^h \qquad \text{for some h,} \qquad (5.2)$$

$$x^h \geq_h \bar{x}^h \qquad \text{for all h.} \qquad (5.3)$$

The description of the model is now complete. For later purposes, we want to add a lemma which is a direct consequence of assumption 2 and will turn out to be central to any characterization of dynamic efficiency for production economies. A firm's profits $p \cdot y^f$ are the sum of two (net-) cash flows: $p_t \cdot y_t^f$ and $p_{t+1} \cdot y_{t+1}^f$. Owing to the model's dynamic nature, profit maximization does *not* imply maximization of each cash flow; quite on the contrary, the first cash flow will normally be negative if there are profitable investment opportunities. But the following can be proven:

Lemma (Cash Flow): The equilibrium cash flow $p_t \cdot \bar{y}_t^f$ of any firm $f \in F_t$ can at most be increased by the amount of the firm's equilibrium investment, i.e. for all $y^f \in Y^f$,

$$p_t \cdot (y_t^f - \bar{y}_t^f) \leq p_t \cdot \bar{k}_t^f. \tag{6}$$

Proof: Using the definition $y_t^f = (s_t^f - k_t^f)$, the firm's cash flow in period t equals $p_t \cdot y_t^f = p_t \cdot s_t^f - p_t \cdot k_t^f$ (profits minus investment). Subtracting the corresponding expression for equilibrium, we obtain

$$p_t \cdot (y_t^f - \bar{y}_t^f) = p_t \cdot (s_t^f - \bar{s}_t^f) - p_t \cdot (k_t^f - \bar{k}_t^f).$$

Due to assumption 2, profit maximization implies maximization of $p_t \cdot s_t^f$. Therefore, $p_t \cdot (s_t^f - \bar{s}_t^f) \leq 0$ and

$$p_t \cdot (y_t^f - \bar{y}_t^f) \leq p_t \cdot (\bar{k}_t^f - k_t^f).$$

From assumption 2, we know that $p_t \cdot k_t^f \geq 0$ which completes the proof. ∎

In reality, a firm has just two opportunities to increase its cash flow. First, it can simply try to make higher profits and second, it can reduce its investment. At equilibrium, however, the first possibility is ruled out by definition so that the cash flow can only be increased via a reduction in investment. Then, the *greatest* possible increase in the current cash flow is given by the *total* amount of investment: the firm can at most invest nothing. Here, assumption 2 plays obviously an important rôle. In a world where current outputs could be produced using future inputs it would be conceivable that a firm's current cash flow can be increased indefinitely. Luckily, such a "substitution against the time axis" can be excluded without substantive loss in generality.

2.2 A General Theorem on Dynamic Efficiency

The following proposition gives a sufficient condition for an equilibrium to be Pareto-optimal. In the proof, assumptions 1 and 2 are employed – and no more premises are necessary. When considering condition (7), observe that the expression $p_t \cdot (\bar{c}_t + \bar{k}_t)$, i.e. consumption plus investment, can be conveniently considered as the present value of national income, evaluated at the original equilibrium. (We recall that prices are never written with a bar, they are always understood as equilibrium prices.) Therefore, the following expression can be interpreted as that fraction of national income which goes to the younger agents.

Theorem 1 (Dynamic Efficiency): A competitive equilibrium $((\bar{x}^h), (\bar{y}^f))$ is Pareto-optimal if

$$\liminf_{t \to \infty} \sum_{H_t} p_t \cdot \bar{c}_t^h + p_t \cdot \bar{k}_t = 0. \tag{7}$$

Proof: Consider another allocation $((x^h), (y^f))$. If this is a Pareto-improvement, we have from (4.1) and (5.1) that $x_t - y_t = \bar{x}_t - \bar{y}_t$, hence $p_t \cdot (x_t - \bar{x}_t) = p_t \cdot (y_t - \bar{y}_t)$ for all t. As a consequence,

$$\sum_{\tau=1}^{t} p_\tau \cdot (x_\tau - \bar{x}_\tau) - \sum_{\tau=1}^{t} p_\tau \cdot (y_\tau - \bar{y}_\tau) = 0. \tag{8}$$

If $((x^h), (y^f))$ is indeed a Pareto-improvement, it follows by a standard argument that $p \cdot \bar{x}^h$ must be increased if household h is to be made better off[1]. By the same token, $p \cdot \bar{x}^h$ may not be decreased for all other households. And for each firm, $p \cdot \bar{y}^f$ cannot be increased because $\bar{y}^f$ is a profit-maximizing production plan. Thus any Pareto-improving allocation is characterized by

$$p \cdot (x^h - \bar{x}^h) = \varepsilon > 0 \quad \text{for some } h \in H_T, \tag{9.1}$$

$$p \cdot (x^h - \bar{x}^h) \geq 0 \quad \text{for all h}, \tag{9.2}$$

$$p \cdot (y^f - \bar{y}^f) \leq 0 \quad \text{for all f}. \tag{9.3}$$

---

1 This is a direct consequence of our assumptions (1.1) to (1.3). For a proof, cf. Debreu (1959, chapter 4).

According to equation (9.1), the household which is made better off has been born in period T. Summing over all h and f yields:

$$\sum_{\tau=1}^{t-1} [\sum_{H_\tau} p \cdot (x^h - \bar{x}^h) - \sum_{F_\tau} p \cdot (y^f - \bar{y}^f)] \geq \varepsilon \quad \text{for all } t > T. \tag{10}$$

Equation (8) depicts what happens in our economy up to period t, whereas equation (10) describes what happens to those households and firms which have been born or founded up to period t-1. Subtracting (10) from (8) we obtain aggregate consumption and production of just those agents who have come into existence in period t:

$$\sum_{H_t} p_t \cdot (x_t^h - \bar{x}_t^h) - \sum_{F_t} p_t \cdot (y_t^f - \bar{y}_t^f) \leq -\varepsilon \quad \text{for all } t > T, \tag{11}$$

so that, multiplying by -1,

$$\sum_{H_t} p_t \cdot (\bar{x}_t^h - x_t^h) + \sum_{F_t} p_t \cdot (y_t^f - \bar{y}_t^f) \geq \varepsilon \quad \text{for all } t > T. \tag{12}$$

Therefore, in every period following T, either the younger households' expenditure must be reduced (left term), or the younger firms' cash flow must be increased (right term). Now, from (1.4) we know that $u_t^h \leq x_t^h$ for all feasible x_t^h, hence by definition (1.5), $\bar{c}_t^h \equiv \bar{x}_t^h - u_t^h \geq \bar{x}_t^h - x_t^h$ and

$$\sum_{H_t} p_t \cdot \bar{c}_t^h \geq \sum_{H_t} p_t \cdot (\bar{x}_t^h - x_t^h) . \tag{13}$$

And from (6) it follows that the said cash flow can at most be increased by the amount of the younger firms' investment

$$\sum_{F_t} p_t \cdot \bar{k}_t^f \geq \sum_{F_t} p_t \cdot (y_t^f - \bar{y}_t^f) . \tag{14}$$

Substituting (13) and (14) into (12) and observing that only the younger firms invest yields

$$\sum_{H_t} p_t \cdot \bar{c}_t^h + p_t \cdot \bar{k}_t \geq \varepsilon \quad \text{for all } t > T. \tag{15}$$

This contradicts condition (7) which basically states that the left-hand expression is *not* bounded away from zero. ∎

During the rest of the present section, we want to interpret and evaluate this theorem. Five assumptions had to be made in order to derive the result. Three of them, namely, convexity of consumption sets (1.1), convexity of preferences (1.2), and local non-satiation (1.3) are also employed in the proofs of the first basic welfare theorem for static equilibrium models. These premises sufficed to derive inequality (12). As has already been pointed out, (12) has the following meaning: In order to arrive at a Pareto-improvement, it must be possible in *every* period following T to reduce the younger households' expenditure or to increase the younger firms' cash flows by at least some number $\varepsilon > 0$.

This is an obvious and nice interpretation, but (12) has the drawback that — when looking at the economy's original equilibrium positition — we cannot pass a judgement about its efficiency: After all, (12) contains variables x_t^h and y_t^f which are *not* evaluated at equilibrium and thus can *a priori* assume any value. And what is more, the terms $(\bar{x}_t^h - x_t^h)$ and $(y_t^h - \bar{y}_t^h)$ can in principle be arbitrarily large. The younger households, for instance, can possibly be forced to work harder and harder so that $(\bar{x}_t^h - x_t^h)$ becomes progressively greater. And such can conceivably be done without hurting them unless specific assumptions about their preferences are made.

This is where our premises (1.4) and (2) come into play. They effectively place bounds on the maximum size of transfers between generations which are feasible within a period. If every consumption-set is bounded from below — so that in particular $x_t^h \geq u_t^h$ for every young household — we immediately obtain inequality (13) which states that the difference $(\bar{x}_t^h - x_t^h)$ can at most equal the households' equilibrium consumption $\bar{c}_t^h$. Similarly, once "substitution against the time axis" is excluded, the firms' current profits can at most be increased by the equilibrium investment $\bar{k}_t^f$, as stated by inequality (14).

Therefore, if the sum of consumption and investment of the *younger* agents, evaluated at equilibrium, vanishes in the limit, it will be impossible to make some household better off without hurting another. Under this condition, we will eventually encounter a generation which cannot be compensated by its children and which therefore has to be made worse off.

2.3 Some Further Results

We now develop two conditions for dynamic efficiency which are easier to grasp, but also more restrictive. These follow, as will be seen, directly from theorem 1.

Corollary 1 (National Income): A competitive equilibrium $((\bar{x}^h), (\bar{y}^f))$ is Pareto-optimal if the present value of national income, written as consumption plus investment, is not bounded away from zero, i.e. if

$$\liminf_{t \to \infty} p_t \cdot (\bar{c}_t + \bar{k}_t) = 0. \tag{16}$$

Proof: The proof is immediate if one realizes that, by definition (1.5), the value of consumption $p_t \cdot c_t^h$ is positive for each household. From (3.1) it follows that the sum in (16) is not smaller than the sum in (7). Therefore, if the former converges to zero, so does the latter. ∎

Condition (16) is usually referred to as the *insignificant future condition*[1] and, for a model with both production and consumption, a special version of it has first been proved by McFadden, Mitra and Majumdar (1980). If the present value of future national incomes becomes "insignificant", that is to say if it is not bounded away from zero, then there is no way to to make anybody better off without making someone else worse off.

In pure production models such as Malinvaud's (1953), the insignificant future condition requires merely that the present value of the equilibrium *capital stock*, $p_t \cdot \bar{k}_t$, is not bounded away from zero. In pure exchange economies, like Samuelson's (1958), efficiency obtains if the present value of equilibrium *consumption*, $p_t \cdot \bar{c}_t$, is not bounded away from zero. In a model with both production and consumption activities, these two conditions have to be fulfilled at the same time, as corollary 1 shows.

---

1 See, for instance, Stephan and Wagenhals (1990). The insignificant future condition has first been used by Malinvaud (1953) in his characterization of efficient intertemporal allocations. Most authors, however, including those mentioned, require that the above present value actually converges to zero. We have just seen that this presumption is too strong: it perfectly suffices that the limit infimum equals zero.

Corollary 2 (Exchange Economy): Assume that there is no production and that households do not supply services:

$$Y^f = \{0\} \quad \text{for all f,} \tag{17.1}$$

$$u^h = 0 \quad \text{for all h.} \tag{17.2}$$

Then, a competitive equilibrium $((\bar{x}^h), (\bar{y}^f))$ is Pareto-optimal if

$$\liminf_{t \to \infty} p_t \cdot \bar{x}_t = 0. \tag{17.3}$$

Proof: Due to (17.1), production drops out of the model and $\bar{k}_t$ vanishes identically. By (1.5), $\bar{c}_t$ equals $\bar{x}_t$ if $u^h = 0$ for all households. Thus, setting $\bar{c}_t = \bar{x}_t$ and $\bar{k}_t = 0$ in (16) proves the claim. ∎

Corollary 2 is a slight generalization of proposition 5.3 from Balasko and Shell (1980) who require the sequence (x_t) to be bounded from above which implies that the economy may not grow permanently. Since, in an exchange economy, $x_t = e_t$ for every t and any feasible x_t, we can say that an equilibrium is dynamically efficient if compound interest eventually exceeds the compound growth of the endowments – but this will be made more precise in a later chapter.

It should be pointed out that there exist economies which violate (16) or (17.3) but display dynamic efficiency via (7). Consider, for instance, an exchange economy where aggregate endowments grow "too fast" but where, at the same time, the younger agents only obtain the minimum feasible consumption (which may or may not be zero). If the equilibrium interest rate falls short of the growth rate we would be inclined to say that the associated path is dynamically inefficient. But beware – as the income of the younger agents is minimal, condition (7) is fulfilled and no Pareto-improvement is possible. Thus, when evaluating dynamic efficiency, it is only the eventual behaviour of the *younger agents'* incomes which has to be taken into account. Whenever their income vanishes in the limit, the equilibrium will be found to be Pareto-optimal. On the other hand, corollaries 1 and 2 are more vivid as compared with our basic theorem and will often be used in the following; the qualification from the last paragraph is not so important for the economies we want to analyze.

2.4 Storable Consumer Goods

Up to here, our analysis contains an implicit assumption which is habitually made in general equilibrium analysis and which is anything but innocuous. The assumption is that all consumer goods are *perishable*, none of them can be stored. To discover such a premise, see, for instance, section 4.3 of Debreu (1959). Debreu requires a consumer's consumption-set to be bounded from below and says that this has an obvious economic justification: For ordinary consumption goods, the lower bound is zero; for labour services, it is a negative real number. This is quite a convincing premise for static economies. As soon as the model is given a *dynamic* interpretation, however, the boundedness assumption becomes questionable.

In order to see this, consider commodity i and assume that it is storable (or durable). A household h which has bought the amount $x_t^{h,i}$ in period t will then be able to sell $x_{t+1}^{h,i} = -x_t^{h,i}$ one period ahead. But this means that, unless we require $x_t^{h,i}$ to be bounded from above, $x_{t+1}^{h,i}$ cannot be bounded from below. Therefore, the seemingly innocent assumption that $x^h \geqslant u^h$ for every feasible commodity bundle x^h is violated in a dynamic model with durable goods.

Storable goods are very important in a model of economic growth because all *assets* (like money or bonds) are among them. Requiring goods to be non-storable effectively rules out households' savings. This is because savings take the following form in our model: Let the i-th commodity be an interest-bearing asset. A household h may acquire $x_t^{h,i} > 0$ units of the asset during its first period of life and sell the same amount $-x_t^{h,i} < 0$ when old. Hence, storable commodities form an important link between the present and the future and assuming them away considerably narrows the scope of the analysis.

Regarding the firms, storability of commodities presents no difficulty whatsoever since storable goods are simply components of the vector k_t^f from assumption 2. But in most of the overlapping-generations literature (see, for instance, Grandmont (1983)) consumer goods are treated in the following manner: First, they are explicitly or implicitly supposed to be perishable; and second, a single commodity – usually referred to as "money" – is introduced which is said to be storable. "Money", then,

2.4 Storable Consumer Goods

displays some "unique features" which will presumably be shared by any other storable commodity. In the present section we want to propose a general definition of storability and show that the conditions for dynamic efficiency which have been derived so far continue to hold in an economy with storable commodities.

Definition (Storable Commodity): Commodity no. i is *storable* for the households if for every t and $h \in H_t$, $u_t^{h,i} = 0$ and

$$x^h \in X^h \quad \text{implies} \quad x_{t+1}^{h,i} \geq -x_t^{h,i} . \tag{18}$$

In this definition, storability is characterized as an objective property of a consumer good: storage of that good must be feasible for every household. Due to our sign conventions, $x_t^{h,i} > 0$ means that household h has bought the amount $x_t^{h,i}$ of commodity i in period t. If so, it is feasible for the household to sell the *same* amount one period ahead. But, and this is important, the household may also dispose of or use up the commodity and sell nothing of it later on. And it is also open to the household to buy again a positive quantity of the good in period t+1. The crucial property of a storable consumer good is that $x_{t+1}^{h,i}$ is *not* bounded from below by a *given* number $u_{t+1}^{h,i}$; the feasible action $x_{t+1}^{h,i}$ depends on which quantity $x_t^{h,i}$ has been chosen one period before.

We could easily extend the definition so as to encompass imperfectly storable goods or "rabbits" if we required $x_{t+1}^{h,i} \geq -\varepsilon \cdot x_t^{h,i}$, where ε is a strictly positive real number. $\varepsilon < 1$ would then indicate an imperfectly storable commodity (like furniture) whereas $\varepsilon > 1$ would hold for "rabbits". A second, but seemingly unrealistic, generalization of (18) would be to allow for storable labour services which are excluded above because $x_t^{h,i}$ has been assumed to be non-negative.

Let us now return to our conditions for dynamic efficiency. Theorem 1 holds obviously in an economy with storable commodities and needs no formal modification, but we have to interpret it a bit differently: The terms $p_t \cdot c_t^h$ now include *savings* as well as consumption of the younger households. If $p_t^i \cdot c_t^{h,i}$ gives the value of a paper asset, for instance, which will be sold by the household in period t+1, we must interpret it as part of the household's savings. Let us conveniently call $p_t \cdot k_t^f$ the *firms' savings*.

Our fundamental condition (7) for dynamic efficiency now requires the infimum of total savings plus the younger households' consumption to vanish in the limit.

At the beginning of this section we have suggested that the second part of the boundedness assumption (1.4) will be violated in an economy with storable goods: x^h_{t+1} cannot be bounded from below unless x^h_t is bounded from above — but there is no reason why the latter should be. Therefore, retaining the definition $c^h = x^h - u^h$, we complete assumption 1 by setting

$$u^{h,i}_{t+1} = -x^{h,i}_t \quad \text{if commodity i is stored by } h \in H_t \,. \tag{1.4'}$$

As a consequence, the households' consumption-sets X^h are no longer bounded from below: If a household buys larger and larger amounts of some storable commodity i in period t, it can decrease $x^{h,i}_{t+1}$ indefinitely. The variable $c^{h,i}_{t+1}$, however, continues to be non-negative because it equals $x^{h,i}_{t+1} - u^{h,i}_{t+1} = x^{h,i}_{t+1} + x^{h,i}_t$. This follows immediately from (18) and (1.4'). Accordingly, $c^{h,i}_{t+1} = x^{h,i}_{t+1} + x^{h,i}_t$ will vanish only if the household sells exactly that quantity in period $t+1$ it has bought in period t. Then, no consumption of commodity i has taken place; the latter has been used as a mere store of value.

These somewhat lengthy considerations are significant for the following reason: In section 2.3, we developed a condition for dynamic efficiency which was much easier to interpret than the supposition of theorem 1: The condition in corollary 1 required the sequence of *national incomes* to vanish in the limit; and in proving it we made use of the fact that the value of everybody's consumption bundle $p_t \cdot c^h_t$ was non-negative. We have just seen that this continues to be so if (1.4') is added to assumption 1. Therefore, corollary 1 and all propositions which will be derived from it later on hold in an economy with storable goods — despite the fact that the consumption bundles are not bounded from below. The expression $p_t \cdot (\bar{c}_t + \bar{k}_t)$ from corollary 1 has now the following meaning:

$p_t \cdot (\bar{c}_t + \bar{k}_t)$ = value of all households' consumption,
+ value of all households' leisure,
+ younger households' savings,
+ younger firms' savings.

In short, $p_t \cdot (\bar{c}_t + \bar{k}_t)$ consists of *total consumption plus total savings* and can conveniently be called national income. This expression slightly exceeds national income in the statistical sense because it includes the value of leisure as well as gross instead of net capital formation – but this should not detain us here. We see that the introduction of storable goods does not raise substantial analytical difficulties but only calls for slightly different interpretations. Theorem 1 and corollary 1 hold in an economy with storable goods, and $p_t \cdot (\bar{c}_t + \bar{k}_t)$ can again be interpreted as national income. There is no point to assume all commodities to be completely perishable.

2.5 The Failure of the First Basic Welfare Theorem

Everybody who is only roughly acquainted with welfare economics knows how extremely simple the proof of the first basic welfare theorem is for models with a bounded horizon. Compared with this well-known proof, the above analysis looks quite involved. In this section we want to address the problem of why the first basic welfare theorem does not hold in the overlapping-generations model. In order to bring out its failure with greatest clarity, we write down the proof of the theorem and then point out those steps which involve a *non sequitur*. In the following, x represents the sequence (x_t), y represents the sequence (y_t) and p represents the sequence (p_t).

Lemma: A competitive equilibrium $((\bar{x}^h), (\bar{y}^f))$ is a Pareto-optimum.

(Erroneous) Proof: Suppose not. Then, there exists a feasible allocation $((x^h), (y^f))$ such that one household is made better off whereas no other household is made worse off:

$$p \cdot x^h > p \cdot \bar{x}^h \quad \text{for some h,} \tag{19.1}$$

$$\text{and} \quad p \cdot x^h \geq p \cdot \bar{x}^h \quad \text{for all h,} \tag{19.2}$$

$$\Rightarrow \quad p \cdot x > p \cdot \bar{x}, \tag{19.3}$$

$$\Rightarrow \quad p \cdot y > p \cdot \bar{y}, \tag{19.4}$$

$$\Rightarrow \quad p \cdot y^f > p \cdot \bar{y}^f \quad \text{for some f,} \tag{19.5}$$

a contradiction to (4.3). ∎

The inequalities (19.1) and (19.2) are correct indeed; cf. the proof of theorem 1. The step from (19.3) to (19.4) is valid only if $p \cdot x$, $p \cdot y$ and $p \cdot e$ converge. Then, the feasibility constraint (5.1), $x-y=e$, requires that $p \cdot y$ rises together with $p \cdot x$. The other two steps involve serious errors.

From the facts that some household's expenditures are increased and that all other households' expenditures are not decreased, we may infer that aggregate household expenditure rises. It does *not* follow, however, that $p \cdot x$ must also rise. This becomes clear as soon as we properly define aggregate household expenditure on the one hand and the the expression $p \cdot x = p_1 \cdot x_1 + p_2 \cdot x_2 + ...$ on the other:

$$\sum_H p \cdot x^h = \lim_{T \to \infty} \sum_{\substack{H_t \\ t<T}} p \cdot x^h, \qquad (20.1)$$

$$\sum_t p_t \cdot x_t = \lim_{T \to \infty} [\sum_{\substack{H_t \\ t<T}} p \cdot x^h + \sum_{H_T} p_T \cdot x_T^h]. \qquad (20.2)$$

From this we see that aggregate household expenditures may differ from the aggregate value of all commodities whilst these two are clearly identical in a model with a bounded horizon. There are two possibilities which invalidate the step from (19.2) to (19.3): First, the above limits may not exist. Second, the right-hand term in (20.2) may be bounded away from zero. In either case, it does not follow from an increase in aggregate household expenditure that the aggregate value of consumption commodities $p \cdot x$ must also rise.

The second error in the above proof is analytically equivalent. Defining aggregate profits on the one hand and $p \cdot y$ on the other we recognize at once that these two may be either infinite or different.

$$\sum_F p \cdot y^f = \lim_{T \to \infty} \sum_{\substack{F_t \\ t<T}} p \cdot y^f, \qquad (21.1)$$

$$\sum_t p_t \cdot y_t = \lim_{T \to \infty} [\sum_{\substack{F_t \\ t<T}} p \cdot y^f + \sum_{F_T} p_T \cdot y_T^f]. \qquad (21.2)$$

In particular, maximization of each profit $p \cdot y^f$ does *not* imply maximization of aggregate profits $p \cdot y$. As a consequence, a rise in $p \cdot y$ does not contradict the profit maximization hypothesis (4.3). We will return to this issue in the appendix to chapter 3.

In a model with a *bounded* horizon, $p_t \cdot x_t$ and $p_t \cdot y_t$ will vanish for all t which exceed some given T_o. The series[1] in (20) and (21) will surely converge and the right-hand expressions in (20.2) and (21.2) will identically vanish from period T_o on. Consequently, the above proof applies and any competitive equilibrium is Pareto-optimal.

The reader should observe that the assumptions $p \cdot x < +\infty$ and $p \cdot y < +\infty$ for all feasible x and y do *not* by themselves entail dynamic efficiency. As a counterexample, the right-hand limit in (21.2) may be negative and bounded away from zero which invalidates the last step in the above proof because $p \cdot y$ can be increased without increasing a single firm's profits[2]. An equilibrium allocation, however, were $p \cdot \bar{x}$ and $p \cdot \bar{y}$ are both finite and were these expressions maximize $p \cdot x$ and $p \cdot y$ for all feasible allocations x and y is often referred to as a *valuation equilibrium*[3]. If a competitive equilibrium is also a valuation equilibrium, it will be Pareto-optimal.

Two decades or so ago there has been a lot of discussion why the first basic welfare theorem fails to hold in economies with an unbounded horizon. This debate had been motivated by Samuelson's (1958) and Diamond's (1965) originally surprising papers; and among the conjectures offered were that in the overlapping-generations model "all souls cannot meet in a single market" (Cass and Yaari (1966)) or that there is a

---

1 By a *series* we always mean an infinite sum. A series is said to converge or to exist if the limit of that sum exists.

2 McFadden, Mitra and Majumdar (1980) claim that $p \cdot \bar{y} < +\infty$ entails Pareto-optimality. But their proof contains an important sign error in their equation (3.12). A simple counterexample to their allegation is the Samuelson (1958) consumption-loan model where $p \cdot \bar{y} \equiv 0 < +\infty$ whilst $p \cdot \bar{x} = p \cdot e$ may diverge.

3 This term has first been introduced by Debreu (1954) whose original definition is more general: Debreu only demands that a linear form be defined on the commodity space which is not necessarily representable as an inner product. Balasko and Shell (1980; 282) rightly think that the "economic justification of this maneuver is questionable".

"double infinity of commodities and agents" (Shell (1971)). Wright (1987) has shown, however, that every equilibrium in the overlapping generations model can be represented as a complete market equilibrium and vice versa. In doing so he has put to rest "the notion that the nonoptimality of some competitive equilibria in overlapping generations economies results from the inability of agents to trade with each other when their lifetimes do not overlap." (p. 200). Shell's "double infinity", on the other hand, may be considered as that property of the model which renders dynamic inefficiency possible. Summing over an infinity of agents and then over an infinity of commodities may yield different values of aggregate consumption, as has been demonstrated above.

2.6 A Stronger Condition

We now derive a stronger condition for dynamic efficiency which will be used repeatedly in the subsequent analysis. It is "stronger" in the sense that we can build economies which violate that condition but meet the prerequisites of theorem 1 and are thus dynamically efficient.

Theorem 2 (Stronger Efficiency Condition): A competitive equilibrium $((\bar{x}^h), (\bar{y}^h))$ is Pareto-optimal if the series of national incomes is finite:

$$\sum_{t=1}^{\infty} p_t \cdot (\bar{c}_t + \bar{k}_t) < +\infty . \tag{22}$$

Proof: Because p_t, $\bar{c}_t$ and $\bar{k}_t$ are all non-negative by definition, condition (22) requires that $p_t \cdot (\bar{c}_t + \bar{k}_t)$ vanishes in the limit. Pareto-optimality then follows from corollary 1. ∎

Theorem 2, when compared with theorem 1, elucidates that we can construct economies with a diverging series of national incomes where the first basic welfare theorem applies nevertheless. Assume, as an illustration, that the present value of national incomes obeys $p_t \cdot (\bar{c}_t + \bar{k}_t) = 1/t$. The associated series obviously diverges; yet the equilibrium is Pareto-optimal as we can infer from corollary 1.

Defining the sequences $c := (c_t)$ and $k := (k_t)$, we may conveniently rewrite (22) as an inner product: $p \cdot (\bar{c} + \bar{k}) < +\infty$. As $p_t \cdot (\bar{c}_t + \bar{k}_t)$ is the present value of national income in period t, is seems appropriate to call the series $p \cdot (\bar{c} + \bar{k})$ the economy's *wealth*. Thus, if an economy's wealth is a real number, then the associated equilibrium will be Pareto-optimal. This condition is much easier to grasp and to interpret than theorem 1. But we must bear in mind that there exist equilibria which violate the requirements of theorem 2, yet can be shown to be Pareto-optimal via theorem 1.

2.7 A Remark on Necessary Conditions

All of the propositions presented above, including theorem 1, give conditions which are sufficient but not necessary for dynamic efficiency. Hence, if any of these conditions appears to be violated one cannot conclude that the path under consideration is dynamically inefficient. Some readers may now ask whether it is possible to derive conditions which are both necessary and sufficient.

Such has in fact been done in the literature for production economies (Cass (1972)) and exchange economies (Balasko and Shell (1980)). These results, however, are rather disappointing — which is not the authors' guilt. In order to derive a necessary criterion for dynamic efficiency one has to make extremely strong assumptions regarding utility and production functions. In particular, it must be assumed that these functions are not only "smooth" but also display curvatures which are uniformly bounded from both above and below.

The intuition behind this requirement is as follows: Consider a path of an exchange economy where $p_t \cdot \bar{x}_t$ is bounded from below by some $\varepsilon > 0$, so that corollary 2 would indicate dynamic inefficiency. The efficiency of this path depends on whether or not $p_t \cdot x_t$ remains to be bounded away from zero after the allocation has been changed slightly from $(\bar{x}_t)$ to (x_t). Roughly speaking, if $p_t \cdot \bar{x}_t \geq \varepsilon$ but $p_t \cdot x_t \to 0$ for *every* other allocation, we would not be surprised to find the original equilibrium to be Pareto-optimal.

To conclude, it is possible to derive necessary conditions for dynamic efficiency. Before this can be done, however, the class of admissible models must be extremely narrowed. Therefore, the conditions are "necessary" in a formal sense only but tell us nothing about economies which do not belong to the remaining class. It is partly for this reason that we have refrained from analyzing necessary conditions. The other, and more important, reason is that the models which will be discussed in a chapter 4 already meet the sufficient conditions – and that is all we need.

2.8 Conclusion

In this chapter the phenomenon of dynamic efficiency has been characterized in a general manner. We have seen that there exist conditions which are rather easy to interpret and which ensure the applicability of the first basic welfare theorem for almost all growth models which have been or might conceivably be developed. The most obvious condition, given in theorem 2, is that the series of national incomes, referred to as the economy's wealth, is a real number. In order to ensure dynamic efficiency, it also suffices to make the weaker assumption that the sequence of national incomes vanishes in the limit, as stated in corollary 1. According to our central result, theorem 1, however, a sufficient condition for dynamic efficiency is that the infimum of the sequence of the younger agents' incomes vanishes eventually.

In order to demonstrate the wide scope of the above analysis, let us give a special example. We assume $\#F_t = 1$ for all t, consumption-sets are bounded from below by **0**, labour supply is exogenous (and modelled as a part of the endowments), preferences and production-sets can be represented by strictly monotonic and strictly quasi-concave utility and production functions, and the latter are also linear-homogenous. Moreover, factors of production are labour and capital (both positive), the entire wage income goes to the younger and the entire interest income goes to the older households, and there are no exogenous endowments except labour. If such an economy's national income – evaluated at the original equilibrium – vanishes in the limit, we can safely conclude from corollary 1 that the path is dynamically efficient. The experienced reader has surely recognized the model just described as a generalized Diamond (1965) model which allows for arbitrarily changing preferences and production functions (technical progress). To obtain the true Diamond model, we have to assume in addition that $\#H_t = (1+g)^t$ for all t and that all utility and productions functions are identical.

The best interpretation of the phenomenon of dynamic inefficiency may be the following which has been proposed in a similar form by Geanakoplos (1987). Consider a *T-truncated economy*: it consists of all households and firms from the sets H_t and F_t, where $t \leq T$, including their endowments. As the agents live for two periods, all economic activities will end after period $T+1$. Now consider the $T+1$-truncated economy. Comparing the two corresponding sets of feasible allocations, we immediately recognize that *more goods* can be handed over to the members of the first T generations; these are the endowments (and working capacities) belonging to the members of generation $T+1$. Hence, the resources which are *socially* available up to any period $T+1$ exceed the resources which are *privately* owned by the agents of the first T generations. Because this holds true for $T \to \infty$, one is tempted to think that every market allocation were inefficient. This is not so, however, since the extra *value* of the additional endowments may vanish in the limit. Thus, if the present value of national income, $p_t \cdot (\bar{c}_t + \bar{k}_t)$, is finite, Pareto-improvements turn out to be impossible.

Chapter 3. Interest and Growth

Since Samuelson's (1958) pioneering paper, the nature of dynamic efficiency has often been characterized in terms of the relationship between the interest rate and the growth rate of national income. This is exactly what we want to do in the present chapter. Such an attempt is not too easy. Many prominent authors in the field, most notably Malinvaud (1953) and Starrett (1970), have argued that in a general equilibrium model of economic growth there is simply no such thing as an interest rate "because own rates of interest differ among commodities and there is no satisfactory aggregation procedure" (Starrett 1970, p. 706). Therefore, conditions for dynamic efficiency which make use of interest and growth rates have only been developed for one-sector (Cass (1972)) or stationary economies (Starrett (1970)) and the profession has refrained from extending these to the general case.

To my mind, this is an overly pessimistic attitude. Our real world is surely neither of the one-sector type nor stationary; yet every layman thinks it apt to speak of "interest rates", which suggests that the latter term must have some meaning. Once we introduce an interest-bearing asset into our model — and it should be clear that, in a model with perfect foresight, there can be only *one* asset — we have a natural definition of interest. We can, then, pose the question whether those interest and growth rates which are actually calculated by our statisticians tell us something about the dynamic efficiency properties of our world (provided we could observe them from now to infinity). This question will soon be answered in the affirmative.

By a *commodity own growth factor* we mean the quantity of the commodity in period t divided by the quantity of the same commodity in period t-1. A *commodity own growth rate* equals the corresponding factor minus one. By a *commodity own interest factor* we mean the exchange ratio between a specific commodity at time t and the same commodity at time t-1. Thus, if a household can exchange a single unit of commodity i at time t-1 for two units of this commodity at time t, the commodity own interest factor equals 2. A *commodity own interest rate* equals the corresponding factor minus one[1]. In the above example, the interest rate equals 1 or 100% per period.

3.1 Commodity Own Rates of Interest

In the present section we employ the basic model from chapter 2 but suppose that there are only two commodities, one of them being a *perishable consumption good* and the other being a *storable asset*. "Assets" have not yet been introduced, therefore we would like to define them at the outset.

Definition (Asset): Commodity no. i is called an *asset* if it is perfectly durable and entirely useless and unproductive. Thus, for all t, households $h \in H_t$ and firms $f \in F_t$ the following holds:

$$x^h \in X^h \quad \text{implies} \quad x_t^{h,i} + x_{t+1}^{h,i} = 0, \qquad (23.1)$$

$$y^f \in Y^f \quad \text{implies} \quad y_t^{f,i} + y_{t+1}^{f,i} = 0, \qquad (23.2)$$

and if two consumption or production plans, respectively, coincide in all other components – i.e. $x_\tau^{h,j} = \bar{x}_\tau^{h,j}$ or $y_\tau^{f,j} = \bar{y}_\tau^{f,j}$ for $\tau = t, t+1$ and all $j \neq i$ – it follows that

$$x^h \in X^h \quad \text{implies} \quad x^h \sim_h \bar{x}^h, \qquad (23.3)$$

$$y^f \in Y^f \quad \text{implies} \quad \bar{y}^f \in Y^f. \qquad (23.4)$$

According to (23.1), a household can choose any positive or negative amount $x_t^{h,i}$ in its first period of life on the condition that a corresponding amount $x_{t+1}^{h,i}$ with the opposite sign is chosen one period later. $x_t^{h,i} < 0$ represents the *issue* of a bond; then $x_{t+1}^{h,i} > 0$ is the *reimbursement*. $x_t^{h,i} > 0$ represents *savings*; then $x_{t+1}^{h,i} < 0$ must be interpreted as *dissavings*. Because the same holds for the firms (with opposite sign conventions) we see that the asset allows a transfer of purchasing power between two subsequent periods. The definition requires also that the quantity of the

---

1 The notion of an "own rate of interest" of a commodity has been introduced by Keynes. For details, see Eatwell (1987) who also points out that this term is used ambiguously in the literature.

asset an agent holds does not directly influence his utility or production possibilities: Every household is indifferent between two commodity bundles which differ only in that they contain different quantities of the asset. And the production possibilities of every firm are perfectly unaffected by the firm's decision on the amount of the asset. Yet, the asset's price may be positive because it allows to shift income between subsequent periods.

Let us move on now to the problem of how to define an *interest rate* in a two commodity-world. The term "strictly positive interest rate" is commonly understood to mean that future consumption goods are cheaper than present consumption goods. What does this imply regarding the behaviour of p_t? The answer is: nothing. For instance, $p_t >> p_{t+1}$ means that the price of *both* the asset and the consumption good decreases from period t to t+1; and this information does not enable us to evaluate the sign of the interest rate.

Let us therefore be more specific about the commodity structure and suppose that the asset is commodity no. 1 whilst the perishable consumption good is commodity no. 2. Under this assumption, we can point out two examples of positive interest:

- A positive rate of interest prevails in period t if $p_t^1 < p_{t+1}^1$ *and* $p_t^2 = p_{t+1}^2$, i.e. if the asset's price increases whereas the consumption good's price remains unchanged. A household, when reducing its demand for the consumption good in period t by Δx_t^2, can afford to buy *more* than Δx_t^2 additional units of the consumption good one period later.

- The interest rate is positive, too, if $p_t^1 = p_{t+1}^1$ *and* $p_t^2 > p_{t+1}^2$, i.e. if the asset's price remains unchanged whereas the consumption good's price decreases. Again, every agent is in a position to exchange Δx_t^2 units of the consumption good in period t for *more* than Δx_t^2 units of the same good in period t+1.

To generalize, our economy displays a positive interest rate if and only if p_{t+1}^1/p_t^1 exceeds p_{t+1}^2/p_t^2 which means that the asset's price rises faster (or declines less fast) than the price of the consumption good. Before it has been specified which goods are assets and which are not, the behaviour the price vector p_t as a whole will not tell us anything about the interest rate.

The problem of defining interest properly should now be plain: When the particular commodity structure of the model at hand is unclear – so that one does not know precisely which commodities are stores of value and which are perishable – it is impossible to infer whether or not an equilibrium price sequence p is associated with positive interest rates. This problem will be overcome in the following section.

3.2 The Asset-augmented Economy

The preceding section has revealed that the concept of "interest" lacks a precise meaning in a model with both storable and perishable commodities. Loosely speaking, a rise in the price of some storable good makes the existence of a positive interest rate more likely whilst a rise in the price of some perishable good makes it less likely; and before it is known precisely which commodities are storable and which are not, nothing definitive can be said about the sign of the interest rate.

In the asset-augmented economy to be developed now, this problem will be solved in a straightforward manner. We simply add an additional commodity no. 0 which is an *asset* in the above sense; but at the same time we retain all definitions and assumptions from the basic model so that, in particular, the abbreviations x^h and y^f are understood *not* to include the asset. Thus there are $n+1$ commodities in our model from now on. Observe that the introduction of only a single asset suffices to define interest if there is no uncertainty. With perfect foresight, all assets of a specific duration would be analytically equivalent in that they would have identical yields.

Definition (Asset-augmented Economy): In addition to the n goods introduced so far, the economy contains an asset in the sense of (23) which will be referred to as commodity no. 0. $(\pi_t^0 | \pi_t)$ is the *original price vector* in period t; it is a point in $\mathbb{R}_{++}^{n+1}$. Associated with it, there is a *derived price vector* $p_t \in \mathbb{R}_{++}^n$ which is defined in the following way:

$$p_t := \left(\frac{\pi_t^1}{\pi_t^o}, \frac{\pi_t^2}{\pi_t^o}, \ldots, \frac{\pi_t^n}{\pi_t^o}\right). \tag{24}$$

The idea behind this definition should be clear. In the asset-augmented economy, an equilibrium price vector $(\pi_t^o | \pi_t)$ is prevailing in every period which, again, contains no explicit information about the interest rate. But here we know commodity no. 0 to be an asset and can conveniently use its price π_t^o in order to normalize the price vector.

Consider some perishable consumption good for which $p_t^i > p_{t+1}^i$. According to (24), the price of this good rises less fast than the asset's price; and we can conclude that its own rate of interest is strictly positive — consumption of the good tomorrow will be cheaper than consumption today.

As a further illustration, consider the two budget constraints of some household $h \in H_t$ which receives no exogenous income from profits or endowments. The household will choose the most preferred commodity bundle subject to the constraints

$$\pi_t^o \cdot x_t^{h,o} + \sum_{i=1}^n \pi_t^i \cdot x_t^{h,i} \leq 0, \tag{25.1}$$

$$\pi_{t+1}^o \cdot x_{t+1}^{h,o} + \sum_{i=1}^n \pi_{t+1}^i \cdot x_{t+1}^{h,i} \leq 0. \tag{25.2}$$

Dividing these equations by π_t^o and π_{t+1}^o, respectively, and using definition (24) we obtain:

$$x_t^{h,o} + \sum_{i=1}^n p_t^i \cdot x_t^{h,i} \leq 0, \tag{26.1}$$

$$x_{t+1}^{h,o} + \sum_{i=1}^n p_{t+1}^i \cdot x_{t+1}^{h,i} \leq 0. \tag{26.2}$$

As the definition (23) of an asset implies $x_t^{h,o} + x_{t+1}^{h,o} = 0$, adding (26.1) and (26.2) yields the household's combined budget constraint $p \cdot x^h \leq 0$, where x^h is understood to include only commodities 1 to n. In a sense, the combined budget constraint $p \cdot x^h$ which has frequently been used in chapter 2 already presupposes the existence of an asset because, without such a store of value, it is difficult for a household to transform present into future consumption or the other way round[1].

Notice that the equilibrium level of $(\pi_t^o | \pi_t)$ is completely indeterminate in each period because a change to $\lambda \cdot (\pi_t^o | \pi_t)$ ($\lambda > 0$) will not change the households' budget sets (or the firms' profits). We could fix the prices π_t^i by introducing *money* into the model but will not do so because we are primarily interested in the real exchange ratios π_t^i/π_t^o, and these are well-defined anyway.

The above definition of an asset-augmented economy is very convenient because, by Walras' Law, we can drop the market for the asset and can entirely forget about the original prices π_t^i. The resulting economy, then, looks exactly like the basic model from chapter 2, the difference being that we can interpret the ratios p_t^i/p_{t+1}^i as commodity own interest factors. Moreover, the p_t^i can be conceived of as *forward prices*. If $p_t^i = $ const. for some commodity i, the forward price of this commodity remains unchanged over time, which means that its *spot price* grows at the rate of interest. As a consequence, the commodity tomorrow is neither cheaper nor dearer than today.

To conclude. In a growth model with both perishable and storable commodities, nothing about the interest rate can be inferred from the behaviour of the original price vector which has been called π_t in the present section. In particular, if all components of the original price vector converge to zero, this will *not* indicate a strictly positive compound rate of interest. Once a particular asset it singled out, however, all prices can be normalized using the price of this asset; and the normalized prices now indicate the exchange ratios between "goods tomorrow" and "goods today". During the rest of our study we will always assume the price vectors p_t to be the outcome of such a normalization.

---

1 Therefore one may well ask whether the ratios p_t^i/p_{t+1}^i can really be interpreted as commodity own rates of interest in an asset-less pure exchange economy like Balasko and Shell's (1980). In that model, a household can only exchange present for future consumption of a specific commodity if it *simultaneously* does the opposite for some other commodity.

3.3 Interest, Growth, and Dynamic Efficiency

According to the above analysis, interest rates can be obtained from the behaviour of the normalized price vector of an asset-augmented economy. Every asset will display the same price behaviour in a world with perfect foresight, but perishable goods, of course, will not. Generally, a different own rate of interest is associated with every perishable good and there exists no adjustment mechanism which equalizes these own rates. In the 1970s, for example, an agent planning the acquisition of a pocket calculator received an implicit interest of far more than ten percent when postponing his purchase for a year, whereas the potential buyer of real estate had to face a small, perhaps even negative, return. This was because pocket calculators' spot prices fell so rapidly during that period whilst the spot value of real estate rose at a rate sometimes exceeding the nominal return on assets.

Such phenomena, it should be emphasized, also occur with perfect foresight, given that different rates of technical progress etc. induce a continuous adjustment in relative prices; and thus every agent faces a different "interest rate" which depends on the composition of the commodity bundle he wishes to acquire in the following period. This will not prevent us from characterizing dynamically efficient paths by means of interest and growth, though. Quite on the contrary, the following simple formulae show that our well-known *statistical* notions of interest and growth facilitate an *exact* evaluation of the efficiency properties of a given growth path — there is no index problem. The idea is to compute *the* growth rate and *the* interest rate as weighted averages of the commodity own growth and interest rates. *Define*

$$\bar{z}_t := \bar{c}_t + \bar{k}_t \tag{27.1}$$

as the equilibrium value of (real) *national income* (written as consumption plus investment; compare section 2.4 for details),

$$G_t := \frac{p_t \cdot \bar{z}_{t-1}}{p_t \cdot \bar{z}_{t-1}} \tag{27.2}$$

as the *real growth factor*, normally calculated as a *Laspeyres quantity index*, and

$$R_t := \frac{p_{t-1} \cdot \bar{z}_t}{p_t \cdot \bar{z}_t} \qquad (27.3)$$

as the *real interest factor* which is simply the ratio of the nominal interest factor and the *Paasche price index* (the latter is normally referred to as the "implicit GNP deflator"). In order to understand the last definition, recall from the preceding section that π_t^0 is the price of the asset whereas $\pi_t = (\pi_t^1,...,\pi_t^n)$ comprises all nominal commodity prices. Then, the *nominal interest factor* is π_t^0/π_{t-1}^0, it displays the increase in the asset's price. The Paasche price index is $\pi_t \cdot \bar{z}_t/(\pi_{t-1} \cdot \bar{z}_t)$ and it is completely indeterminate as is the nominal interest factor because our model contains no money. Forming the ratio of the nominal interest factor and the Paasche price index immediately yields (27.3) since $p_t^i := \pi_t^i/\pi_t^0$, and this real interest factor is well-defined in equilibrium.

Corollary 3 (Interest, Growth, and Dynamic Efficiency): A competitive equilibrium $((\bar{x}^h), (\bar{y}^f))$ is Pareto-optimal if the compound interest rate eventually exceeds the compound growth rate, i.e. if

$$\liminf_{t \to \infty} \prod_{\tau=2}^{t} \frac{G_\tau}{R_\tau} = 0. \qquad (28)$$

Proof: From definitions (27.3) and (27.2) it follows immediately that

$$\frac{G_\tau}{R_\tau} \equiv \frac{p_\tau \cdot \bar{z}_\tau}{p_{\tau-1} \cdot \bar{z}_{\tau-1}}. \qquad (29)$$

Hence, for every $t \geq 2$,

$$\prod_{\tau=2}^{t} \frac{G_\tau}{R_\tau} \equiv \frac{p_t \cdot \bar{z}_t}{p_1 \cdot \bar{z}_1}, \qquad (30)$$

where $p_1 \cdot \bar{z}_1$ is a given positive number. Condition (28), therefore, is equivalent to the requirement that the limit infimum of $p_t \cdot \bar{z}_t$ itself vanishes. Due to definition (27.1), $p_t \cdot \bar{z}_t$ is identical to $p_t \cdot (\bar{c}_t + \bar{k}_t)$, and thus condition (28) together with corollary 1 implies that the equilibrium is Pareto-optimal. ∎

Corollary 3 characterizes dynamically efficient growth paths in terms of *compound* interest and growth rates. For some purposes, it may be convenient to think of *geometric averages* instead and to say that efficiency obtains if the interest rate exceeds the growth rate on the average. This is indeed true but overly restrictive: Denoting the product term in (28) by μ_t (and forgetting about the infimum for a moment), our efficiency criterion requires $\mu_t \to 0$ whilst an interpretation in terms of geometric averages demands that the t-th root of μ_t vanishes in the limit, and this is a stronger requirement. As an example, assume that μ_t equals 0.5^t for all t. The associated sequence (μ_t) vanishes in the limit whereas the t-th root constantly equals 0.5 and is thus bounded away from zero. At the theoretical level, it is therefore preferable to employ compound instead of average interest and growth rates.

3.4 Conclusion

In the present chapter, dynamically efficient growth paths have been characterized in terms of the eventual behaviour of interest and growth rates. Our central result, given in corollary 3, generalizes and confirms a proposition which has been developed for either one-sector or stationary economies by various authors (mentioned in the introduction to this chapter): A competitive equilibrium will be found to be dynamically efficient if the compound interest rate exceeds the compound growth rate in the limit. For the sake of empirical content, real interest and growth rates have been defined in the statistical sense (using those Laspeyres and Paasche indices which are actually employed in order to calculate them).

It turned out that the statistical figures – imperfect as they are in other respects – really suffice to determine the efficiency of a known growth path. This result has much to do, of course, with the purely qualitative character of our efficiency conditions; they do not raise an index problem.

One final remark. A glance at definitions (27.2) and (27.3) shows that in the above analysis real growth and real interest factors have been defined as the corresponding nominal factors times the *same* price index (i.e. the implicit GNP deflator). The reader may feel, therefore, that there is a more direct way to empirically assess the efficiency of a given growth path, namely, to employ nominal instead of real interest and growth factors. This is right provided that nominal equilibrium prices are fixed through some monetary institution. In this case, define

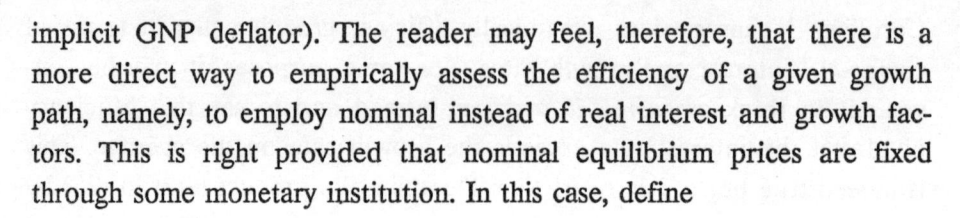

$$G_t^n := \frac{\pi_t \cdot \bar{z}_t}{\pi_{t-1} \cdot \bar{z}_{t-1}} \tag{31.1}$$

as the *nominal growth factor* and

$$R_t^n := \frac{\pi_t^o}{\pi_{t-1}^o} \tag{31.2}$$

as the *nominal interest factor* (remember that π_t^o represents the asset's money price in period t). Now, definition (24) ($p_t^i := \pi_t^i/\pi_t^o$) immediately entails

$$\frac{G_\tau^n}{R_\tau^n} \equiv \frac{p_\tau \cdot \bar{z}_\tau}{p_{\tau-1} \cdot \bar{z}_{\tau-1}}, \tag{32}$$

which corresponds to equation (29), and the proof of corollary 3 goes through without any further modification. In short, we may directly compare nominal growth and interest factors in order to evaluate the efficiency of our monetary economies.

Appendix: The Cash Flow Criterion

In this appendix we want to sketch the so-called cash flow criterion for dynamic efficiency. Such a condition has recently been proposed as a substitute for the interest and growth rates criterion by Abel, Mankiw, Summers and Zeckhauser (henceforth: Abel et al.) in their 1989 paper. These authors argue that, in a stochastic setting, the marginal productivity of capital rather than the safe real interest rate must be used in order to assess the efficiency of actual growth paths. The marginal productivity, however, depends on accounting conventions and is difficult to measure; therefore, it would be preferable to use the cash flow of the firm sector instead.

Putting uncertainty aside, we want to show how the cash flow criterion fits into the present model of economic growth. In doing so, it will be convenient to introduce the following terminology: If aggregate equilibrium profits $p \cdot \bar{y}$ are finite and maximized over all feasible $p \cdot y$, we say that the firm sector is operating *dynamically efficient*; if not, we say that the firms are *accumulating too much*. Thus, only the efficiency of the firm sector will be considered throughout the appendix; and we must bear in mind that "overall ineffiency" can also have other causes — such as initial endowments which grow "too fast".

Assumption (Constant Returns to Scale): For all firms f and every real number $\lambda \geq 0$,

$$y^f \in Y^f \quad \text{implies} \quad (\lambda \cdot y^f) \in Y^f. \tag{33}$$

According to a standard argument, constant returns to scale imply that profits vanish in equilibrium. Hence, in periods $t = 1, 2, \ldots$, the following will hold for each firm:

$$p \cdot \bar{y}^f \equiv p_{t+1} \cdot \bar{y}^f_{t+1} + p_t \cdot \bar{y}^f_t = 0, \tag{34}$$

$$\Leftrightarrow p_{t+1} \cdot \bar{y}^f_{t+1} = -p_t \cdot \bar{y}^f_t \geq 0. \tag{35}$$

The last equation means that any firm's future returns equal the value of its capital stock, both expressed as present values. In order to see this, observe that the right-hand side may be re-written as $p_t \cdot \bar{k}^f_t - p_t \cdot \bar{s}^f_t$, were $\bar{k}^f_t$ and $\bar{s}^f_t$ are defined in assumption 2. Profits from static production vanish in equilibrium, so $-p_t \cdot \bar{y}^f_t$ equals the value of the capital stock which, according to assumption 2, is non-negative.

In period t, the *equilibrium market value* of the newly founded firms equals the present value of the firms' net revenue in period $t+1$, or, via (35), the value of the accumulated capital stock:

$$\bar{V}_t := \sum_{F_t} p_{t+1} \cdot \bar{y}^f_{t+1}. \tag{36}$$

The equilibrium *cash flow* of all firms operating in period t is simply given by $\bar{D}_t := p_t \cdot \bar{y}_t$. Because outputs are denoted with a positive sign and inputs with a negative sign, $\bar{D}_t > 0$ indicates that the firms operating in period t produce more value than they consume. In a model without exogenous endowments, $\bar{y}_t$ equals $\bar{x}_t$ and we may express $\bar{D}_t$ as $p_t \cdot \bar{x}_t$. The interpretation is obvious: $p_t \cdot \bar{x}_t > 0$ means that the household sector consumes more value than it produces.

Using definition (3.2), the equilibrium cash flow becomes

$$\bar{D}_t := p_t \cdot \bar{y}_t \equiv \sum_{F_{t-1}} p_t \cdot \bar{y}_t^f + \sum_{F_t} p_t \cdot \bar{y}_t^f . \tag{37}$$

The sum's left-hand term will normally be positive whereas the right-hand term will be negative; but the sign of $\bar{D}_t$ is indeterminate. Adopting the convenient terminology of Abel et al. (1989), the firm sector may either be a *net spout* ($\bar{D}_t > 0$) or a *net sink* ($\bar{D}_t < 0$).

Proposition (Cash Flow Criterion): If $\bar{D}_t/\bar{V}_t \geq \varepsilon > 0$ for all t, the firm sector is operating efficiently. But if $\bar{D}_t/\bar{V}_t \leq -\varepsilon < 0$ for all t, the firms are accumulating too much.

Proof (Efficiency): Substituting $\bar{D}_t$ and $\bar{V}_t$ from (37) and (36),

$$\frac{\sum_{F_{t-1}} p_t \cdot \bar{y}_t^f + \sum_{F_t} p_t \cdot \bar{y}_t^f}{\sum_{F_t} p_{t+1} \cdot \bar{y}_{t+1}^f} \geq \varepsilon > 0 \tag{38}$$

by hypothesis so that, using (35)

$$\frac{\sum_{F_{t-1}} p_t \cdot \bar{y}_t^f}{\sum_{F_t} p_{t+1} \cdot \bar{y}_{t+1}^f} \geq 1 + \varepsilon > 1. \tag{39}$$

The sequence of the returns $p_{t+1} \cdot \bar{y}_{t+1}^f$ of all firms which have been founded in period t thus vanishes in the limit and, using equality (35) again, we also obtain:

$$\lim_{t \to \infty} \sum_{F_t} p_t \cdot \bar{y}_t^f = 0 . \tag{40}$$

Combining equations (21.1) und (21.2), we know that aggregate equilibrium profits $p \cdot \bar{y}$ equal

$$p \cdot \bar{y} = \sum_F p \cdot \bar{y}^f + \lim_{t \to \infty} \sum_{F_t} p_t \cdot \bar{y}_t^f . \qquad (41)$$

Because, according to (40), the right-hand side converges to zero and because profits $p \cdot \bar{y}^f$ vanish for all except for those firms founded in period 0, we finally obtain a real number which maximizes $p \cdot y$:

$$p \cdot \bar{y} = \sum_{F_0} p_1 \cdot \bar{y}_1^f . \qquad (42)$$

(Inefficiency): If $\bar{D}_t / \bar{V}_t \leq -\varepsilon < 0$, the expression in (39) will be smaller than $1-\varepsilon$ so that the associated sequence approaches minus infinity. And (41) implies that $p \cdot \bar{y} = -\infty$, too. Therefore, aggregate profits can surely be increased by setting $y^f = 0$ for all firms, which implies $p \cdot y = 0 > -\infty$. ∎

The crucial point in the proof was to show that the the right-hand term in (41) vanishes. If so, individual profit maximization entails aggregate profit maximization and the firms operate efficiently.

As an illustration, consider Diamond's (1965) steady state model with a constant interest rate r and a constant rate of population growth g. Capital profits in period t are given by $\pi_t = r \cdot K_{t-1}$ and investment equals $I_t = g \cdot K_{t-1}$ because, along a steady state path, the constant capital labour ratio must be preserved. The undiscounted *cash flow* $\pi_t - I_t$ amounts to $(r-g) \cdot K_{t-1}$ and is positive if the interest rate exceeds the growth rate. This corresponds to the ordinary criterion for dynamic efficiency. Expressing the cash flow as a present value like in our above analysis and setting $K_t = (1+g)^t \cdot K_0$, aggregate profits are given by the following expression:

$$\sum_{t=1}^{\infty} \bar{D}_t = \sum_{t=1}^{\infty} \frac{\pi_t - I_t}{(1+r)^t} , \qquad (43)$$

$$= (r-g) \cdot K_0 \cdot \sum_{t=1}^{\infty} \left[\frac{1+g}{1+r}\right]^{t-1} . \qquad (44)$$

Assume $r>g$: Then, the last expression converges to $(1+r)\cdot K_o$ which corresponds to (42) in that aggregate profits (or cash flows) equal the profits of the old firms in period 1. Assume $r<g$: Then, the expression in (A.12) will approach minus infinity, indicating dynamic inefficiency.

Chapter 4. An Economy with Land

In the present chapter we want to introduce *land* into our growth model in order to show its relevance for the issue of dynamic efficiency. Such an attempt may appear somewhat far-fetched at first, because land is not a standard ingredient of growth models. There exists, of course, a vast variety of *spatial*, static models with land which are chiefly employed in the field of urban economics. But concerning *dynamic* theory, it is, indeed, very hard to find models with land even in the macroeconomic literature. Among the articles I encountered are Calvo (1978) who has shown that land can entail indeterminacy of equilibrium, and Feldstein (1977a) who has analyzed the incidence of a tax on pure rent.

On the other hand, there seems to be a common belief that, in a *steady state*, where some *exogenously* given rent grows at the rate g, the real interest rate must be greater than g. Since it is evidently difficult, however, to reconcile the notion of a steady state (with *constant* factor proportions) with the assumption of a non-growing productive factor as land (implying *changing* factor proportions) the literature has not considered such an argument important. A notable exception is McCallum (1987) who analyzed a steady state model with Cobb-Douglas production and utility functions and demonstrated that the model's equilibria must be dynamically efficient[1].

Our aim, now, is the following: Using a *non-steady state* approach we want to show that, under a mild regularity assumption, the existence of non-reproducible productive goods rules out inefficient growth paths: competitive equilibria are Pareto-optimal[2].

---

1 Contrary to McCallum's own view, however, his argument does not necessarily hold in a broader class of models, as has been shown in an interesting paper by Rhee (1991).

2 From a purely analytical viewpoint, Scheinkman (1980) is another predecessor of our approach. He has argued that share trading rules out inefficiency, and his firm's shares are analytically similar to what we call land. Scheinkman does not employ our regularity assumption (see theorem 3) because he implicitly considers a non-growing economy.

4.1 A Characterization of Land

There are several features which distinguish land from any other commodity. First, the economy is exogenously endowed with land at the inception of time; there is no need to produce it. Second, the given quantity of land cannot be augmented by households or firms; whenever a household or a firm supplies a certain quantity of land, it must have bought that quantity before. Third, and most important, land is durable in the following sense. When a household or a firm uses a specific portion of land for some reason or another, it will be able to sell exactly the same portion at a later point in time. To sum up, land need not be produced, cannot be reproduced, and is perfectly durable.

This general description of land, it is to be noted, does not rely on any notion of "usefulness" or "productivity": we will simply call a commodity "land" if it meets the three above requirements. Now, there are very many different types of land in reality which can be specified properly by their location and the time index. As n is the total number of commodities available in every period, our model possibly contains $1 \leqslant n$ varieties of land. But, as will become clear later, our analysis only presumes that there is one type of land. By suitably renumbering the commodities, we can always assume that land is the *first component* of the commodity vector. This does not imply that the 2nd, 3rd etc. components are *not* land; it is simply immaterial whether they are land or not.

The following definition summarizes this characterization of land.

Definition (Land): Commodity no.1 is called *land* if it is supplied by nature in a constant amount, if it cannot be produced, and if it is not used up during consumption or production. Thus the following holds for all t, households $h \in H_t$ and firms $f \in F_t$:

$$e^1 = (\ell, 0, 0, ...) \quad \text{where } \ell > 0, \tag{45.1}$$

$$x^h \in X^h \quad \text{implies} \quad x_t^{h,1} \geqslant 0 \quad \text{and} \quad x_t^{h,1} + x_{t+1}^{h,1} = 0, \tag{45.2}$$

$$y^f \in Y^f \quad \text{implies} \quad y_t^{f,1} \leqslant 0 \quad \text{and} \quad y_t^{f,1} + y_{t+1}^{f,1} = 0. \tag{45.3}$$

Note that at time $t=1$, there are also old households and firms which have been born or founded in period $t=0$. We could have assumed equally that the total amount of land is the property of these old agents, but that would have complicated our notation without changing the results. Hence, equation (45.1) states that the total amount of land (of a certain quality) is among the exogenous endowments, whereas (45.2) and (45.3) — together with our convention $x_o = y_o = 0$ — imply that the said old agents have no land.

Let us have a closer look at equation (45.2). It says that a young household can only buy land: $x_t^{h,1} \geq 0$, i.e. land is not among the services supplied by households. When old, the household can sell land in exactly the same quantity it has bought one period before: $x_t^{h,1} + x_{t+1}^{h,1} = 0$, i.e. land is perfectly durable. Equation (45.3) is analogous but contains a "$\leq$" instead of "$\geq$" since the firms' inputs are written with a negative sign. Thus, a firm cannot produce land but only sell land in just the amount it has bought one period before. As usual, we also assume that households and firms can freely dispose of land if p_{t+1}^1 happened to be non-positive. In simpler terms, equations (45) state that land is neither an agent's net input nor a net output. This is exactly what we mean when saying that land cannot be produced and is perfectly durable.

To summarize, an economy under consideration is an *economy with land* if it is possible, by suitably renumbering the commodity indices, to meet equations (45). Other components of the commodity vector may be land in the above sense as well, but whether they are or not is perfectly immaterial to our further analysis.

4.2 Land as a Consumption Good

All commodities which are "land" in the literal sense are consumption goods of the utmost importance. This may be made precise in the following manner: Consider the commodity bundle x^h of some household h, let the vector ϱ^h include all commodities which meet definition (45), and set $\varrho^h = 0$. It is immediately clear, then, that the household will die; every man needs some space in order to survive.

But this somewhat dramatic scenario should not obscure the fact that, among the commodities defined by equations (45), some are not land in the literal sense. Think, for instance, of a picture by Rembrandt. Such a picture, once it has been painted, need not be produced, cannot be reproduced, and is perfectly durable — and is thus "land".

The following definition makes precise what we mean by saying that land is "useful": We compare two commodity bundles which differ only in containing different quantities of land and then assume that the household will prefer the bundle which contains more land.

Definition (Useful Land): Land is *useful* for household $h \in H_t$ if more consumption of land is always feasible for and preferred by this household. Thus, if $\bar{x}^h \in X^h$ and $x^{h,i}_\tau = \bar{x}^{h,i}_\tau$ for $\tau = t, t+1$ and $i = 2 \ldots n$, then

$$x^{h,1} > \bar{x}^{h,1} \quad \text{implies} \quad x^h \in X^h \quad \text{and} \quad x^h >_h \bar{x}^h . \tag{46}$$

In order to find land to be useful for at least one household, we possibly have to renumber the commodity indices appropriately. Assume, for instance, that commodity no. 1 is a square yard in the sahara which is, indeed, land in the sense of our definition. If no household happens to desire such a location we can exchange indices 1 and, say, 2337 if commodity no. 2337 is a square yard on Manhattan Island.

We now give an obvious (if not trivial) lemma which nevertheless is central to the derivation of our central result.

Lemma 1 (Price of Useful Land): If, in period t, land is useful for at least one household $h \in H_t$, its equilibrium price obeys

$$p^1_t - p^1_{t+1} > 0 . \tag{47}$$

Proof: Recall from definition (45.2) that $x^{h,1}_t \geq 0$ and $x^{h,1}_{t+1} = -x^{h,1}_t$. Therefore,

$$p^1_t \leq p^1_{t+1} \quad \text{implies} \quad p^1_t \cdot x^{h,1}_t + p^1_{t+1} \cdot x^{h,1}_{t+1} \leq 0 . \tag{48}$$

Now, for any feasible consumption plan $\bar{x}^h$, there exists another feasible plan x^h with more land which is strictly preferred to $\bar{x}^h$, cf. equation (46). If (48) holds, the preferred plan does not cost more: $p \cdot x^h \leq p \cdot \bar{x}^h$, so the demand for land is unbounded and there exists no equilibrium consumption plan. ∎

For example, if $p_t^1 = p_{t+1}^1$, the household can buy arbitrarily large amounts of land without violating its budget constraint. Because more land is always preferred, the household's demand for land is unbounded, and an equilibrium does not exist. The lemma basically states that the land's services must have a strictly positive price. This price, however, is not p_t^1 but $p_t^1 - p_{t+1}^1$ since, after having used land for a while, the household can re-sell it at the prevailing price p_{t+1}^1.

In this section we have seen how the notion of useful land can be rigorously formulated. For later purposes, the section contains only one important result. It is that, if land is useful for at least one household born in period t, the land's forward price must strictly decrease during that period.

4.3 Land as a Factor of Production

There is no need to stress the importance of land as a factor of production. In fact, it was no accident that the classical economists, when delineating the triad of factors of production, always spoke of "land, labour and capital" and not, in alphabetical order, of "capital, labour and land". The significance of land is most obvious for agriculture; but land is also indispensible for manufacturing, and even universities (who need teaching rooms) and software engineers (who need places for their computers) cannot produce anything without using some land.

Basically, land is called "productive" if the use of more land either facilitates increasing some output or enables the firm to diminish some other input. In what follows we characterize productivity in purely technical terms, using production-sets.

Definition (Productive Land): Land is *productive* for firm $f \in F_t$ if the use of more land is feasible and allows the firm to increase some output or to diminish some other input. Thus, for every $\bar{y}^f \in Y^f$ there exists some $y^f \in Y^f$ such that

$$y_t^{f,1} < \bar{y}_t^{f,1} \quad \text{and} \quad y_\tau^{f,i} \geq \bar{y}_\tau^{f,i}. \tag{49}$$

for $\tau = t, t+1$ and all $i = 2...n$, the right-hand inequality being strict for at least one τ and i.

Again, we will often be forced to renumber the commodity indices suitably if commodity no.1 is to be productive in this sense. Today, for instance, condition (49) is unlikely to hold for any firm if a square yard on the moon (which is land) has been chosen as commodity no.1. But, after appropriately redefining indices, condition (49) appears to be rather weak.

We now give a lemma which closely resembles lemma 1 of the preceding section. Taken together, these two show that the price of land must follow a rather strict rule once land is found to be either useful or productive.

Lemma 2 (Price of Productive Land): If, in period t, land is productive for at least one firm $f \in F_t$, its equilibrium price obeys

$$p_t^1 - p_{t+1}^1 > 0. \tag{50}$$

Proof: Consider the firm's equilibrium production plan $\bar{y}^f \in Y^f$. According to (49), there exists another feasible plan y^f with the following property: $p_\tau^i \cdot y_\tau^{f,i} \geq p_\tau^i \cdot \bar{y}_\tau^{f,i}$ for $\tau = t, t+1$ and all $i = 2...n$, the inequality being strict for one τ and i. Now suppose that, contrary to the above assertion, $p_t^1 - p_{t+1}^1 \leq 0$. Then, the premise $y_t^{f,1} < \bar{y}_t^{f,1}$ together with the fact that $y_t^{f,1} = -y_{t+1}^{f,1}$ holds for all feasible y^f (cf. definition (45.3)) implies

$$p_t^1 \cdot y_t^{f,1} + p_{t+1}^1 \cdot y_{t+1}^{f,1} \geq p_t^1 \cdot \bar{y}_t^{f,1} + p_{t+1}^1 \cdot \bar{y}_{t+1}^{f,1}. \tag{51}$$

Thus, each component of $p \cdot y^f$ weakly exceeds the corresponding component of $p \cdot \bar{y}^f$, and the excess is strict in at least one instance. Therefore, the production plan $\bar{y}^f$ is not profit-maximizing and cannot be an equilibrium production plan. ∎

Suppose, for example, that $p_t^1 = p_{t+1}^1$. The firm can then buy arbitrarily large amounts of land in the first period, planning to sell them for the same price in the second period. In doing so, profits can be made arbitrarily large when land is a productive input; hence the firm's demand for land is unbounded and an equilibrium does not exist. This is the decisive feature of land as a factor of production: The use of land is costly only if its price tomorrow will be smaller than its price today.

The lesson of this section is similar to that of the preceding section.

Whenever there is one type of land which is productive for at least one firm, the land's forward price must strictly decrease during the period under consideration.

4.4 The Land's Income Share

In order to prepare the ground for our central result, which will be given in the next section, we want to introduce the notion of *rent* and the *land's income share*. What is "rent" in a general equilibrium model? The answer is as follows:

$$\text{Rent:} \quad \varrho_t := p_t^1 - p_{t+1}^1. \tag{52}$$

A rent is the price an agent must pay when using a certain type of land (commodity no. 1) for one period. We are using the term "rent" here in the sense of the classical economists who distinguished three varieties of income: wage income, interest income, and rent income. In reality there exist two completely separate markets for land – a fact which may obscure the appropriateness of definition (52):

– First, there is a *stock market* for land, the property market. A buyer, after paying p_t^1, obtains the ownership of a certain quantity of land.

– Second, and apparently quite remote, there exists a *rental market* for land on which the buyer, after having paid the rent, obtains the right to use a certain quantity of land for a specified time.

Yet, it is easily seen that the following two contracts are analytically equivalent: A tenant can either pay $1.000 to the landlord as an annual rent; or he can buy the piece of land for $p_t^1 = \$11{,}000$ and *simultaneously* sell it forward to the landlord for $p_{t+1}^1 = \$10{,}000$. Thus, a tenancy agreement is nothing but a spot contract combined with a forward contract. And the rent, ϱ_t, just equals the difference between the forward prices p_t^1 and p_{t+1}^1.

The meaning of lemmas 1 and 2 becomes now obvious: If land is useful or productive, the right to employ it for one period must cost something, i.e. the rent must be strictly positive. And using (52), equations (47) and

(50) in fact both state that $\varrho_t > 0$ in every period when land is either useful or productive. As a trivial consequence, p_t^1 will also be positive because we admitted free disposal of land.

Recall that in equation (45.1), the real number $\ell > 0$ has been defined as the total amount of land of a specific quality. Thus $\varrho_t \cdot \ell$ is the total expenditure on land in period t or, what amounts to the same, the rent income in period t. The expression $p_t \cdot (\bar{c}_t + \bar{k}_t)$ denoting national income in period t, the land's income share is simply the ratio of these two variables:

$$\text{Land's income share:} \quad \frac{\varrho_t \cdot \ell}{p_t \cdot (\bar{c}_t + \bar{k}_t)} = \frac{\text{Rent income}}{\text{National income}} > 0 . \quad (53)$$

This definition does, of course, not correspond to the statistical concept of the land's income share because the latter encompasses rents paid for *all* types of land whilst expression (53) gives only the rent paid for a *specific location* as a fraction of national income. The inequality sign in (53) follows from our above lemmas which both state that $\varrho_t > 0$. Together with $\ell > 0$ and the fact that national income can never be negative, it follows that the land's income share is a strictly positive number in every period where land is either useful or productive.

4.5 Land and Dynamic Efficiency

In chapter 2 we discussed the possibility of dynamically inefficient growth. It turned out that even in the most competitive of all worlds, individually rational behaviour will not rule out such an occurence. Thus the first basic welfare theorem does not apply to exchange and production economies with an unbounded horizon. We want to show now that this pessimistic picture changes drastically if the presence of land is given explicit attention: Land qualitatively alters the efficiency properties of a competitive economy. In claiming this, however, one difficulty must be taken into account: On a purely formal level, it would be possible that land, though useful or productive, becomes *asymptotically irrelevant* in the sense that the land's income share *vanishes in the limit* (though we have just seen that it is always strictly positive). In this case, land would virtually drop out of the model and we were left with the results known so far. This is due to the already mentioned fact that the model's efficiency properties depend only on the *eventual* behaviour of the variables. Therefore, it is assumed in the following theorem that the land's income share is not only strictly positive but also bounded away from zero by an arbitrarily small number.

Theorem 3 (Land and Dynamic Efficiency): Assume that land is useful or productive in every period, and that its equilibrium income share is bounded away from zero:

$$\frac{\varrho_t \cdot \ell}{p_t \cdot (\bar{c}_t + \bar{k}_t)} \geq \varepsilon > 0 \quad \text{for all t.} \tag{54}$$

Then, the equilibrium is Pareto-optimal.

Proof: If land is either useful or productive, lemmas 1 and 2 imply the sequence $p^1 = (p_1^1, p_2^1, ...)$ to be monotonically decreasing and bounded from below by zero, hence converging. But every converging sequence is a Cauchy sequence, i.e. $\varrho_t = p_t^1 - p_{t+1}^1$ vanishes in the limit.

As ℓ is constant, the numerator in (54) will vanish also, and so must the denominator because the ratio is bounded away from zero. But owing to corollary 1, $p_t \cdot (\bar{c}_t + \bar{k}_t) \to 0$ guarantees Pareto-optimality. ∎

Let us shortly analyze this proof. When establishing lemmas 1 and 2 we utilized the perfect durability of land; this sufficed to ensure that any equilibrium price sequence $(p_1^1, p_2^1, ...)$ must be decreasing and that the rent is strictly positive. The proof of the theorem additionally requires the total amount of land (ℓ) to be constant or, at least, non-increasing. (Our proposition would not hold for "rabbits".) Thus, all of the characteristic features of land, summarized in definition (54), are necessary and sufficient for the above result.

Assumption (54) appears to be very weak because it requires the existence of only *a single* type of land whose income share does not vanish in the limit. It may well be that (54) is violated for many inferior plots of land; but our result obtains once there is at least one square yard – say, in the center of Tokyo – which does not become irrelevant in the far future. The virtue of theorem 3 and the underlying model is that they minimize the assumptions necessary for proving that dynamic inefficiency is ruled out in an economy with land. On the other hand, we can claim by no means that the above proof is intuitively appealing. It simply does not bring out properly the forces which are preventing the economy from accumulating "too much". A more vivid description of these forces will be given in a later chapter.

4.6 A Stronger Efficiency Result

In section 2.5 we presented another sufficient condition for dynamic efficiency which is overly strong but much easier to interpret: An equilibrium is Pareto-optimal if the infinite series of national incomes converges. What we want to do in the present section is to show that an economy with land also fulfills this stronger condition. To be more specific, we do not need to make any further assumptions but only have to exploit the information which is already contained in the notion of useful or productive land.

Lemma 3 (Series of Rents): If land is useful or productive in every period, the series of rents converges to a strictly positive number:

$$0 < \sum_{t=1}^{\infty} \varrho_t < +\infty . \tag{55}$$

Proof: Using the definition $\varrho_t = p_t^1 - p_{t+1}^1$ of the rent, the first t-1 terms of this sum read

$$\varrho_1 + \varrho_2 + \ldots + \varrho_{t-1} = (p_1^1 - p_2^1) + (p_2^1 - p_3^1) + \ldots + (p_{t-1}^1 - p_t^1) = (p_1^1 - p_t^1) . \tag{56}$$

Taking the limit for t→∞ immediately establishes the claim because $p_1^1 > p_t^1 > 0$ holds for all periods t and every equilibrium price sequence p. ∎

This lemma resembles an assertion which is often made in fincance and capital theory. It is said that, when there exists a good which yields pure rent forever, the rate of interest must exceed the growth rate if that good is to have a finite value. Our lemma shows how this claim follows from individual optimization – provided we interpret interest and growth rates

4.6 A Stronger Efficiency Result

as *commodity own* interest and growth rates. The crucial part in the proof is that p_t^1 does not approach minus infinity, but that is a direct consequence of the free-disposal assumption.

From (56) we see that the series of rents equals p_1^1 if p_t^1 vanishes in the limit. This has an obvious interpretation: When the terminal value of land is zero, the sum of discounted rents simply equals the land's current price. If the terminal value of land is positive, however, the sum of discounted rents falls short of the land's current price. In either case, this sum is a strictly positive real number.

Theorem 4 (Stronger Efficiency Result): Assume that land is useful or productive in every period, and that its income share is bounded away from zero:

$$\frac{\varrho_t \cdot \ell}{p_t \cdot (\bar{c}_t + \bar{k}_t)} \geq \varepsilon > 0 \quad \text{for all t.} \tag{57}$$

Then, the series of national incomes converges, and the equilibrium is Pareto-optimal.

$$\sum_{t=1}^{\infty} p_t \cdot (\bar{c}_t + \bar{k}_t) < +\infty, \tag{58}$$

Proof: From lemma 3 it follows immediately that

$$\sum_{t=1}^{\infty} \varrho_t \cdot \ell/\varepsilon < +\infty. \tag{59}$$

But from (58) we have

$$p_t \cdot (\bar{c}_t + \bar{k}_t) \leq \varrho_t \cdot \ell/\varepsilon \quad \text{for all t,} \tag{60}$$

which proves that the series of national incomes converges. Theorem 2 then states that any equilibrium is Pareto-optimal. ∎

We can thus conclude: Whenever land is useful or productive and does not drop out of the model eventually, the series of national incomes is a real number. In order to arrive at this stronger result, no more assumptions had to be made.

4.7 Conclusion

The present chapter has revealed that in an economy with land the series of national incomes is a real number. Or, which means basically the same, the real interest rate exceeds the real growth rate in the long run. Moreover, the first basic welfare theorem applies. Evaluating the premises that have been made in order to establish this result, I personally believe that the assumptions which underly the whole theory of general equilibrium are much more restrictive than the requirements that land (i) exists, (ii) is either useful or productive, and (iii) will not become perfectly irrelevant in the far future. But no more was needed in the derivation of theorem 3.

The political implications of the above analysis, especially for fiscal policy and the design of social security systems, are far-reaching. As has been pointed out in the introduction to this chapter, most authors who dealt with the issue of dynamic efficiency have not found it advisable to include land into their models. It is no surprise, then, that they often passed rather pessimistic judgements on the efficiency of the market system. Cass (1972), for instance, states at the end of his pioneering paper:

"The possibility of such errant behaviour has to do with the fact that there's neither a market signal nor a market adjustment mechanism [which ensures dynamic efficiency]. This means that the only way a wealthy economy with a strong Protestant-type ethic can avoid overaccumulation is by conscious government policy" (p. 220).

And when facing a situation where the interest rate falls short of the growth rate, Cass "wouldn't hesitate pressing for a much less expansionary growth policy" (p.221), i.e. for government debt. In view of the above results, such a position must be seriously questioned for at least two reasons.

First, as will become clear later, the phenomenon of dynamic inefficiency has nothing to do with a Protestant-type ethic, i.e. with a high propensity to save. An economy with land will display dynamically efficient growth however high the stock of wealth may be which is accumulated in equilibrium. Intuitively, whenever the interest rate tends to fall short of the

4.7 Conclusion

growth rate, the agents will be inclined to buy land instead of real capital. The price of land, and thus the consumption of those agents who sell land, will be bid up whereas the stock of productive capital will be reduced. This is an automatic adjustment mechanism which prevents the economy from accumulating "too much".

Second, it is perfectly possible even in an economy with land that the interest rate is smaller than the growth rate for a long while (but not permanently). Yet, such an occurence would be no indication of dynamic inefficiency because, for the latter, it is only the eventual behaviour of the economy that counts. Hence one would be seriously mistaken if pressing for higher government debt as soon as the growth rate happens to exceed the interest rate.

To conclude, the above analysis suggests that there exists in fact an automatic adjustment mechanism — i.e. the price of land — which prevents the economy from accumulating "too much". So, if I continue to fear dynamic inefficiency, this is rather due to the fact that our real markets are not perfectly competitive.

Chapter 5. Exhaustible Resources

In reality we find commodities which have very much in common with land: Nature endowes us with these commodities, we cannot produce them, and they are durable at least in the sense that they can be stored costlessly; moreover, many of them have turned out to be useful or productive. We are talking here, of course, about *exhaustible resources* — like oil or gas.

Because of the many similarities between land and exhaustible resources it seems natural to ask whether or not the latter will also prevent dynamic inefficiency. This will be analyzed first. As a second theme, we know from the literature that in a perfectly competitive economy there exists the danger of *underutilization* of a resource: Even when perfect foresight prevails, it is possible that a certain fraction of the resource stock will never be used. Does this sort of dynamic inefficiency fit into our basic model or is it an independent phenomenon which must be given a special treatment? In order to answers these questions we need an exact characterization of "exhaustible resources" which will be offered in the opening section.

5.1 A Characterization of Exhaustible Resources

As has already been mentioned in the introduction to this chapter, exhaustible resources can be distinguished from other commodities by the following features: First, we are exogenously endowed by nature with these resources. Second, they cannot be produced by households or firms. Observe that it would not matter if it were possible to produce *substitutes* for the resources which are identical in a technical sense: this would not prevent us from distinguishing, for instance, commodity no. 303 (oil) and commodity no. 4711 (synthetic oil). And finally, resources are durable in the restricted sense that they can be stored costlessly. Hence — are exhaustible resources analytically equivalent with land? The following definition suggests that the answer is in the negative.

Definition (Exhaustible Resource): Commodity no.2 is called an *exhaustible resource* if it is supplied by nature in a constant amount, if it cannot be produced, and if it can be stored costlessly. Thus the following holds for all t, households $h \in H_t$ and firms $f \in F_t$:

$$e^2 = (S_1, 0, 0, \ldots) \quad \text{where } S_1 > 0, \tag{61.1}$$

$$x^h \in X^h \text{ implies } x_t^{h,2} \geq 0 \text{ and } x_t^{h,2} + x_{t+1}^{h,2} \geq 0, \tag{61.2}$$

$$y^f \in Y^f \text{ implies } y_t^{f,2} \leq 0 \text{ and } y_t^{f,2} + y_{t+1}^{f,2} \leq 0. \tag{61.3}$$

Furthermore, define $\sigma = (0, \varepsilon, 0, \ldots, 0 | 0, -\varepsilon, 0, \ldots, 0)$ as the *storage vector*. Then, for any $\varepsilon > 0$,

$$x^h \in X^h \text{ implies } (x^h + \sigma) \in X^h \text{ and } (x^h + \sigma) \sim_h x^h, \tag{61.4}$$

$$y^f \in Y^f \text{ is equivalent to } (y^f - \sigma) \in Y^f. \tag{61.5}$$

Here, S_1 is the entire *stock* of, say, oil of a specific quality and location; again, the old agents living in period 1 have nothing of if. The exhaustible resource is not among the services offered by households, and whenever a household sells some amount of the resource, it must have bought this amount before; cf. equation (61.2). Moreover, the firms cannot produce the exhaustible resource, and any firm which sells some amount of the resource must have bought that amount before; cf. equation (61.3).

There is only a minor, yet crucial, difference between definitions (45) and (61). In the present definition, we require $x_t^{h,1} + x_{t+1}^{h,1}$ and $y_t^{f,1} + y_{t+1}^{f,1}$ to be non-negative and non-positive, respectively; whereas in (45) these sums were supposed to vanish. The interpretation is obvious and at the same time important: A young household which has bought some oil can either burn it or store it in the cellar and sell it at a later date. And a firm may either use oil as a productive input or may sell it later on. Here we recognize a feature which distinguishes exhaustible resources from land. The resource can be *either* used *or* stored, whereas land can be used *and* stored at the same time. To put it another way, the utility or productivity of an exhaustible resource is indispendibly related to its *destruction*.

Finally, consider the meaning of (61.4) and (61.5). We have said above that a resource can be stored costlessly. The owner of an ore mine, for instance, can simply do nothing and leave the ore in the ground. In the above definition, a vector σ is used which has been called the *storage vector*. The 2nd component of σ equals ε, the n+2th component equals $-\varepsilon$, and all other components are zero. Thus, a commodity bundle $x^h + \sigma$ differs from x^h only in that more of the resource is stored by household h. And $y^f - \sigma$ differs from y^f only in that more of the resource is stored by firm f. Definition (61.4) states that an increase in storage is always feasible for a household and will not change the household's utility. According to definition (61.5), storage of the resource is always feasible for a firm and will not change the firm's other production possibilities: It is technically possible for a firm to drop the storage from $y^f - \sigma$ and simply produce y^f.

To conclude, an economy under consideration is an *economy with an exhaustible resource* if, after having suitably renumbered the commodity indices, commodity no.2 meets the above definition. Other components of the commodity vector may be exhaustible resources as well, this is immaterial. It is also immaterial whether or not commodity no.1 is land in the sense of the foregoing chapter.

5.2 Exhaustible Resources as Consumption Goods

Our definition of an exhaustible resource merely stated that production of this resource is infeasible, that the resource can be stored costlessly, and that nature supplies a positive stock of it. We now turn to the interesting cases where the resource is either useful or productive. "Usefulness" will be defined in the following manner: We compare two commodity bundles which differ only in containing different quantities of the resource and then assume that the household will prefer the bundle which allows greater consumption of the resource.

Definition (Useful Exhaustible Resource): An exhaustible resource is *useful* for household $h \in H_t$ if more consumption of it is always preferred by the household. Thus, if $x^h, \bar{x}^h \in X^h$ and $x^{h,i}_\tau = \bar{x}^{h,i}_\tau$ for $\tau = t, t+1$ and all $i \neq 2$,

$$x^{h,2}_t + x^{h,2}_{t+1} > \bar{x}^{h,2}_t + \bar{x}^{h,2}_{t+1} \quad \text{implies} \quad x^h >_h \bar{x}^h . \qquad (62)$$

Recall that the exhaustible resource has been defined as commodity no.2. x^h and $\bar{x}^h$ are two commodity bundles which differ only in the 2nd and the n+2th component. Consequently, $x_t^{h,2}$ is the household's demand for the resource in period t, and $x_{t+1}^{h,2}$, if negative, is the household's supply of the resource in period t+1. In order to understand the definition, the reader should realize that *consumption of the resource* is given by $x_t^{h,2} + x_{t+1}^{h,2}$ and not by $x_t^{h,2}$. This is because the household has two possibilities: After purchasing some amount $x_t^{h,2} > 0$, it can either *store* the resource and sell it one period ahead, then $x_t^{h,2} + x_{t+1}^{h,2} = 0$. Or the household can *consume*, i.e. destroy, the resource, then $x_t^{h,2} + x_{t+1}^{h,2} > 0$.

Our definition of an exhaustible resource already implied that more storage of the resource is feasible for and will not hurt the household. It is open to the household, for instance, to buy an ore deposit, leave it unchanged, and give it away at a later date. Or the household can store oil in its cellar without burning is. To do such things is feasible but does not make oneself feel better off.

Therefore, equation (62) states that the household will prefer the consumption bundle x^h to $\bar{x}^h$ only if it allows greater consumption of the resource. And consumption, to repeat, always means destruction of the resource. This distinguishes the resource from land. Comparing (62) and (46) shows that more land does in fact increase the household's utility notwithstanding that the amount of land obtained is entirely given away one period later.

To summarize, an exhaustible resource is useful for a household if the consumption of the resource makes the household better off. However, the household may also store the resource costlessly; and such storage will not affect the household's utility.

5.3 Exhaustible Resources as Factors of Production

Let us turn now to the notion of a productive resource. The latter will be characterized in a manner which parallels the definition of productive land; cf. section 4.3. Thus, an exhaustible resource is said to be a "productive" input if its destruction enables the firm to increase some output or to decrease some other input.

Definition (Productive Exhaustible Resource): An exhaustible resource is *productive* for firm f∈F_t if the use of a greater portion of the resource is feasible and allows the firm to increase some output or to diminish some other input. Thus, for every $\bar{y}^f \in Y^f$ there exists some $y^f \in Y^f$ such that

$$y_t^{f,2} + y_{t+1}^{f,2} < \bar{y}_t^{f,2} + \bar{y}_{t+1}^{f,2} \quad \text{and} \quad y_\tau^{f,i} \geq \bar{y}_\tau^{f,i} \tag{63}$$

for $\tau = t$, $t+1$ and all $i \neq 2$, the right-hand inequality being strict for at least one τ and i.

The exhaustible resource has been defined as commodity no.2 in definition (61). We already know that mere storage of the resource is costless but will not affect a firm's other production possibilities. The *use* of the resource by a firm equals $-(y_t^{f,2} + y_{t+1}^{f,2})$ which gives, for instance, the amount of oil that has been burned in the production process. Now consider (63). The left-hand inequality states that, starting from some feasible production plan $\bar{y}^f$, there exists another feasible plan y^f in which a greater quantity of the exhaustible resource is used (destroyed). And according to the right-hand inequality which is strict for at least one other commodity, the new plan y^f enables the firm to produce more outputs using less other inputs.

To summarize, a firm for which the exhaustible resource is a productive input has two possibilities. The firm can either store the resource or it use it as a true input. In the former case, other production possibilities are unchanged. But if a greater portion of the exhaustible resource is actually used, the firm can either increase some output or reduce some input.

5.4 The Hotelling Rule

Before we can answer the questions which have been posed in the introduction to this chapter we want to derive a rule which is known as the *Hotelling rule* in the exhaustible resources literature. To do so is not only interesting in itself. We will soon realize, indeed, that the Hotelling rule is the central key for saying something about the efficiency properties of an economy with exhaustible resources.

Lemma 4 (Hotelling Rule): Whenever, in equilibrium, an agent stores a strictly positive amount of the exhaustible resource, the resource's forward price must remain constant. Thus, for all t and any $h \in H_t$ or $f \in F_t$,

$$\bar{x}^{h,2}_{t+1} < 0 \quad \text{implies} \quad p^2_t = p^2_{t+1}, \tag{64.1}$$

$$\bar{y}^{f,2}_{t+1} > 0 \quad \text{implies} \quad p^2_t = p^2_{t+1}. \tag{64.2}$$

Proof for Households: Observe first that the household is indifferent between $\bar{x}^h$ and a commodity bundle without storage which can be constructed by setting $x^{h,2}_{t+1} = 0$ and $x^{h,2}_t = \bar{x}^{h,2}_t + \bar{x}^{h,2}_{t+1}$. This is because storage yields no direct utility, cf. equation (61.4). Now, if $p^2_t > p^2_{t+1}$, the commodity bundle without storage were cheaper so that $\bar{x}^h$ would not be an equilibrium. But if $p^2_t < p^2_{t+1}$, the household would increase the storage indefinitely. Therefore, p^2_t equals p^2_{t+1}.

Proof for Firms: Observe first that the firm's profits from buying and selling commodities other than the resource remain unchanged if we set $y^{f,2}_{t+1} = 0$ and $y^{f,2}_t = \bar{y}^{f,2}_t + \bar{y}^{f,2}_{t+1}$. This is because mere storage is not productive, cf. equation (61.5). Now, if $p^2_t > p^2_{t+1}$, the production plan without storage were more profitable so that $\bar{y}^f$ would not be an equilibrium. But if $p^2_t < p^2_{t+1}$, the firm could make arbitrarily large profits by increasing the storage indefinitely. Therefore, p^2_t equals p^2_{t+1}. ■

The Hotelling rule, though analytically trivial, is a deep and valuable proposition if considered from an economic perspective. It facilitates a sharp charaterization of the price behaviour of an exhaustible resource which does not rely on any notion of usefulness or productivity. Whenever the resource is voluntarily held by an agent, its present value must remain constant. In an economy with a uniquely defined interest rate, the spot price of the resource must therefore grow at the rate of interest. This is the more familiar version of the Hotelling rule.

In the lemma, *storage* has been defined as follows: A household h stores some amount of the resource if and only if $x^{h,2}_{t+1} < 0$ which implies $x^{h,2}_t > 0$. The latter inequality cannot be used to characterize storage because the household may use up $x^{h,2}_t$ completely. By the same token, $y^{f,2}_t < 0$ means that a firm has bought a certain quantity of the resource, but this does not imply storage because the resource may be completely destroyed in the production process. $y_{t+1}^{f,2}>0$, however, ensures that the firm has stored this latter quantity.

In concluding, we want to emphasize again that the Hotelling rule has nothing to do with usefulness or productivity of an exhaustible resource — it would also apply to goods which are completely useless (like "money"), provided that these goods are held voluntarily by the agents. In the above proof we only make use of the fact that the resource can be stored costlessly. The Hotelling rule sharply distinguishes exhaustible resources from land as can be seen by comparing lemma 4 with lemmas 1 and 2: The forward price of useful or productive land must strictly decrease whereas the forward price of an exhaustible resource — useful and productive or not — will remain constant.

5.5 Exhaustible Resources and Dynamic Efficiency

Will the presence of exhaustible resources preclude dynamic inefficiency? This question is suggested by the many similarities between land and exhaustible resources, and by the fact that, in section 4.5, we observed land to prevent an economy from accumulating "too much" indeed. After the foregoing characterization of an exhaustible resource, it is not difficult to answer the question.

To begin with, we define the total *stock of the resource* at the beginning of period t:

$$S_t := \sum_{H_t} c_t^{h,2} + \sum_{F_t} k_t^{f,2}. \tag{65}$$

The resource stock at time t equals total purchases of the resource by the younger households and the younger firms. Our characterization of an exhaustible resource implies $c_t^{h,2}=x_t^{h,2}$ if we assume it to be feasible for a household to have nothing of the resource ($u_t^{h,2}=0$). It is also clear that the resource is among the capital goods because $k_t^{f,2}>\bar{k}_t^{f,2}$ facilitates $y_{t+1}^{f,2}>\bar{y}_{t+1}^{f,2}$. Recall our convention $k_t^{f,2}=-y_t^{f,2}$ which ensures that all purchases of the resource are written with a positive sign.

Surely, if the resource is to prevent dynamic inefficiency, we must have $\bar{S}_t > 0$ for all t, $\bar{S}_t$ denoting the *equilibrium* stock. For suppose that the resource is used up completely in finite time so that $\bar{S}_t = 0$ for all $t > T$. Redefining the time index by setting $T = 0$ we were then left with an economy without an exhaustible resource, knowing that such an economy is liable to grow inefficiently. Therefore, $\bar{S}_t$ and thus $\bar{S}_{t+1}$ must be strictly positive in every period $t = 1, 2, \ldots$, i.e. in every period some agent must voluntarily hold a certain amount of the resource. But now,

$$\bar{S}_{t+1} > 0 \quad \text{implies} \quad p_t^2 = p_{t+1}^2, \tag{66}$$

as we infer from the Hotelling rule (64). This is because $\bar{S}_{t+1} > 0$ implies that either $\bar{x}_{t+1}^{h,2} < 0$ for some household or $\bar{y}_{t+1}^{f,2} > 0$ for some firm: If, in equilibrium, the agents from generation $t+1$ can buy positive quantities of the resource, the resource must have been stored voluntarily by the agents from generation t. The Hotelling rule confirms that this is only possible if the forward price of the resource remains unchanged during period t.

As a consequence, exhaustible resources *will not prevent dynamic inefficiency*. In order to realize this, recall our proof of theorem 3 where land had been shown to guarantee dynamic efficiency. In this proof, we repeatedly made use of the fact that total income from land is a stricly positive and strictly decreasing sequence

$$(p_t^1 - p_{t+1}^1) \cdot \ell > 0. \tag{67}$$

Land was hence shown to have a strictly positive own rate of interest exceeding the land's own rate of growth (which was zero). By contrast, an analogous equation for the exhaustible resource reads

$$(p_t^2 - p_{t+1}^2) \cdot \bar{S}_{t+1} \equiv 0, \tag{68}$$

implying that the resource yields no *rent* in the sense we have been using the term "rent". But in section 4.5 it was precisely the existence of a rent which rendered dynamically inefficent paths impossible.

To summarize, there are two cases: Either the resource drops out of the model: $\bar{S}_t = 0$ for $t > T$ so that we are left with an economy without an exhaustible resource. Or the resource will not be used up in finite time, then its own rate of interest must vanish identically. In both cases, dynamic inefficiency is perfectly possible: National income may or may not converge to zero; there is no regulating mechanism which forces it to do so. The economic intuition behind this result is that the resource yields no rent, which is ultimately due to the fact that it cannot be stored and used at the same time.

5.6 Efficient Use of Exhaustible Resources

The problem we want to analyze now is harder than the question answered in the preceding section. And it is only fair to say that no convincing answer to it has been offered as yet. The problem is this one: Under which circumstances will a resource be used efficiently in a competitive economy with an unbounded horizon? Two prominent authors in the exhaustible resources field, viz. Dasgupta and Heal (1979), have made the following claim:

Lemma 5 (Necessary Condition for Efficient Use): If there exists one household $h \in \mathbb{N}$ for which the resource is useful, the following must hold if an equilibrium is to be Pareto-optimal

$$\lim_{t \to \infty} \overline{S}_t = 0. \qquad (69)$$

Proof: Suppose that, on the contrary, the sequence $(\overline{S}_t)$ is bounded away from zero: $\overline{S}_t \geq \varepsilon > 0$. Then, we may construct another *feasible* sequence (S_t) by setting $x_t^{h,2} = \overline{x}_t^{h,2} + \varepsilon$ and $x_{t+1}^{h,2} = \overline{x}_{t+1}^{h,2}$ for the above household and reducing $\overline{S}_\tau$ by ε in every subsequent period $\tau > t$. From (62) we infer that household h is hereby made better off. On the other hand, (61.4) and (61.5) imply that the other households' utilities as well as the firms' profits remain unchanged. Thus, the original allocation is Pareto-inefficient. ∎

Condition (69) simply requires that a *useful* resource is completely exhausted in the limit. The same would hold for a *productive* resource, provided that an increase in some firm's profits could be used to make some household better off. Because in the preceding section we have shown exhaustible resources not to prevent dynamic inefficiency, there are three conceivable possibilities. Either a resource is used up in finite time, or it is used up in the limit, or it is never used up altogether. The latter occurence is dynamically inefficient if the resource is useful for at least one household.

Employing corollary 1, we can derive a sufficient condition for the efficient use of a resource: Equation (16) states that an equilibrium is Pareto-optimal if the limit infimum of $p_t \cdot (\overline{c}_t + \overline{k}_t)$, the present value of national income, is zero. Assume that such is true for all commodities i≠2, i.e. for all commodities except the exhaustible resource. Then, from the definition of the inner product, it follows trivially that

$$\lim_{t \to \infty} p_t^2 \cdot \overline{S}_t = 0 , \qquad (70)$$

is a *sufficient* condition for dynamic efficiency. $\overline{S}_t$, as defined in (65), is simply the missing second term in (16). We have substituted "lim" for "lim inf" here because both p_t^2 and $\overline{S}_t$ are monotonic sequences. Therefore, efficient use of a resource is guaranteed if the present value of the remaining resource stock vanishes in the limit.

For purely logical reasons, we now encounter the following problem: Condition (70) is *sufficient* for an efficient use of the resource whereas condition (69) is *necessary*. Therefore, (70) has to imply (69) — but from a mathematical viewpoint it is difficult to see why it should do. To put it in more vivid terms: Conditions like (70) are widely used in general equilibrium analysis and are commonly understood to state something like "the interest rate exceeds the growth rate". On the other hand, conditions like (69) are encountered in the exhaustible resources literature, and they are interpreted as a *special* requirement which applies to resources only. As an immediate consequence, some authors seem to think that the presence of exhaustible resources raises *additional* problems regarding the efficient use of supply — problems, which are not encountered in economies with produced goods only. The following theorem suggests that this is a misleading view.

Theorem 5 (Efficient Use of a Resource): If the exhaustible resource (commodity no.2) is useful for at least one household h∈ℕ, then

$$\lim_{t\to\infty} p_t^2 \cdot \overline{S}_t = 0 \quad \text{implies} \quad \lim_{t\to\infty} \overline{S}_t = 0. \tag{71}$$

Proof: The only critical case is that p_t^2 converges to zero whereas $\overline{S}_t$ does not. Therefore, we only have to show that

$$\lim_{t\to\infty} p_t^2 = 0 \quad \text{implies} \quad \lim_{t\to\infty} \overline{S}_t = 0, \tag{72}$$

if the resource is useful for at least one household h. Suppose that, on the contrary, $\overline{S}_t \geq \varepsilon > 0$. Because in every period some agent must voluntarily store the resource, p_t^2 will remain constant according to the Hotelling rule. This means that, if p_t^2 converges to zero, the sequence (p_t^2) must vanish identically: $p_t^2 \equiv 0$. The household h for which the resource is useful could thus have had more consumption of it without spending more. Therefore, $\overline{S}_t$ cannot be an equilibrium. ∎

The following lesson can be drawn from this theorem: *Underutilization* of a resource is not a separate phenomenon but only a special case of *overaccumulation*, which is to say that these seemingly remote phenomena have a common underlying structure. An economy with an exhaustible resource is neither more nor less apt to display dynamic inefficiency, and it would be misleading to say that the competitive mechanism, presumably performing well with respect to capital accumulation, fails to allocate exhaustible resources efficiently. In fact, the market may fail in both cases, and exhaustible resources do not introduce novel difficulties. The presence of (non-irrelevant) land, however, ensures efficient resource utilization in the same fashion as it prevents overaccumulation.

The above analysis also confirms a conjecture from Dasgupta and Heal (1979). According to these authors, efficient use of an exhaustible resource implies that (i) the resource's price obeys the Hotelling rule and (ii) the resource will be completely used up in finite time or in the limit. They then guessed these two conditions to be also *sufficient* for efficiency "at least for some simple economies" (p. 218). Such is indeed true even in the *general* case: If $\overline{S}_t$ converges to zero, (70) will certainly be fulfilled and the equilibrium is Pareto-optimal (provided, of course, that the other commodities also meet the prerequirement of corollary 1): As the resource's equilibrium forward price is a constant real number (Hotelling rule), p_t^2 cannot approach infinity, and $\overline{S}_t \to 0$ is equivalent to $p_t^2 \cdot \overline{S}_t \to 0$.

5.7 Conclusion

In the present chapter we have shown that exhaustible resources, if properly defined, fit well into the basic model from chapter 1. These resources are similar to land in several respects but there is one important difference: Land can be stored and used — as a consumption good or as a factor of production — simultaneously whereas exhaustible resources cannot. As an immediate consequence, land must bear a rent in equilibrium, implying that its forward price strictly decreases. The forward price of a resource, by contrast, will remain constant, which is the basic meaning of the Hotelling rule. As regards dynamic inefficiency, exhaustible resources will not prevent such an occurence; it is absolutely possible that an economy with exhaustible resources accumulates "too much". And what is more, these resources are themselves liable to being used inefficiently. Perfect competition and perfect foresight will not preclude underutilization of a resource. But, as I have argued in the last section, underutilization of exhaustible resources and overaccumulation of capital are analytically equivalent and there is no *a priori* reason to believe that the presence of exhaustible resources raises additional dangers of an inefficient use of supply. In an economy with land (which does not become irrelevant in the limit), underutilization of exhaustible resources is ruled out anyway.

Chapter 6. Examples and Applications

Here the closing chapter of our study begins whose contents, as has been indicated in the introduction, will be more vivid and tractable than the theory developed so far, if also much more special. No new proposition will be derived. No attempt at generalizing the previous ones will be made. The stress will be on interpretation and evaluation. Each of the following sections is self-contained so that readers who are in a hurry may pick the topics they are most interested in and can skip other sections without loss of continuity.

The models to be analyzed in the sequel differ from those above in two respects. First, they are all *macroeconomic*. In my view, macroeconomic analysis rests on the premise that many phenomena from reality would also occur in a world with only a single commodity and only one type of households, usually referred to as the representative household. Such a presumption is obviously reasonable for phenomena as inflation and certainly inadequate for sectoral allocation problems. The preceding models may be considered as a microeconomic foundation of what follows.

Second, as a matter of mere convenience, we will use *spot prices* instead of future prices from now on. This makes the notation more intelligible and will hardly cause confusion since, in a model with a single produced consumption commodity only, there is no need to write down the commodity's price explicitly; the latter will simply be used as the numéraire. For the relative spot prices of land, exhaustible resources and the like new symbols will be introduced in order to prevent confusion with the previous notation.

6.1 Dynamic Efficiency in a Simple Growth Model

In the present section we want to develop a simple growth model in order to demonstrate the nature and causes of dynamic inefficiency in as expressive a manner as possible. Instead of using forward prices, efficient paths will be directly characterized in terms of the relationship between interest and growth rates. To begin with, however, a look at the existing literature on dynamic efficiency seems to be useful. In reviewing this field, Boadway (1989; 19) states that "It is also in many ways an incomplete literature" because the results are derived from rather special models, most notably one-sector economies without production or pure exchange economies. Let us discuss some results in chronological order.

1. (Phelps 1965): Consider the steady state of an economy which grows at a rate g; the interest rate may be r. The steady state is dynamically efficient if and only if r⩾g.

Thus, if r<g the economy is trapped in an inefficient state. Because r is a decreasing function of the capital stock K, this case has also been referred to as "overaccumulation". The most striking example of overaccumulation is a path where in every period the whole output is invested so that the associated consumption path vanishes identically. It is obviously possible here to increase the utility of at least one generation without hurting other generations.

2. (Cass 1972): A necessary condition for dynamic inefficiency is

$$\prod_{\tau=1}^{\infty} f'(k_\tau) = 0 \, ,$$

where $f'(k_\tau)$ is the marginal productivity of capital in period τ.

In Cass's model, it is to be noted, inefficiency means that it is possible to have more *consumption* in every period rather than more *utility*. According to this definition, Samuelson's (1958) consumption-loan model would always entail efficiency because total consumption in any period equals the sum of the given endowments. In what he believes to be a "complete characterization" of the problem, Cass employs very special assumptions: The capital stock must be bounded from below by a strictly positive number, the marginal productivity of capital must be bounded from above, and a maximum maintainable capital stock has to exist.

3. (Balasko-Shell 1980): A sufficient condition for dynamic efficiency is

$$\liminf_{t \to \infty} p^t = 0 \, ,$$

where p^t is the price of the good in period t, measured in units of the good in period 1. Clearly, this implies $p^1 := 1$.

Balasko and Shell's theorem applies to a pure exchange economy with perishable goods only, exogenous endowments, and no capital accumulation. The sequence of endowments must be bounded from above so that permanent growth at a constant positive rate is ruled out. The proposition thus says that, with a declining price of the commodity, the rate of interest must be positive (i.e. exceed the growth rate which is non-positive).

4. (Spremann 1984): In a small open economy facing given interest factors R_t and given growth factors G_t, a competitive allocation is dynamically efficient if and only if

$$\inf \{G_1/R_1,\ G_1G_2/R_1R_2,\ G_1G_2G_3/R_1R_2R_3,\ ...\} = 0,$$

provided that the relative sizes of transfers between generations are bounded from above by some real number $h > 0$.

Spremann's condition is both sufficient and necessary because interest and growth factors are constant in a neighborhood of the equilibrium — due to his assumption of a small open economy. This premise also forces him to place an *a priori* bound upon the transfers' relative sizes. Such a bound need not be introduced if we consider closed economies where the national product serves as a natural upper bound. Owing to the small economy assumption, Spremann's model differs from the models considered before, and in a sense complements them.

These four results on dynamic efficiency, though derived from completely different models, are remarkably similar. And, what is more, the proofs also have very much in common. In all cases an essential assumption is that transfers between generations (which possibly entail Pareto-improvements) are bounded from above in some way or another. These similarities suggest that the models have a common underlying structure so that it is possible to derive a more general condition for dynamic efficiency — a conjecture that proved true in chapter 2 whose central result (theorem 1) encompasses all the above approaches as special cases.

Let us now introduce the perhaps simplest model which facilitates analyzing the nature of dynamic inefficiency. The model can be thought of as a reduced form of a competitive economy; it has the following characteristics. First, there is an exogenous sequence (Y_t) of strictly positive *national incomes* which implies a sequence of strictly positive *real growth factors*, $G_t := Y_t/Y_{t-1}$. Second, in every period $t \in \mathbb{N}_0$ a utility-maximizing agent is born who lives in periods t and $t+1$ and obtains a specific fraction of total national income. His utility function $U_t(c_t^1, c_{t+1}^2)$ ($U_t: \mathbb{R}_+^2 \to \mathbb{R}$) is strictly monotonically increasing and quasi-concave. And third, we suppose the existence of a perfectly competitive capital market where the agents can exchange period t consumption for period $t+1$ consumption at the endogenously determined rate R_{t+1}, the latter being an *interest factor*. In equilibrium, R_{t+1} equals $(\partial U_t/\partial c_t^1)/(\partial U_t/\partial c_{t+1}^2)$, the agent's marginal rate of substitution: In every period, the representative agent adjusts his marginal rate of substitution between present and future consumption to the interest factor.

Now, considering the original allocation, what can be done in order to achieve a Pareto-improvement? As income is exogenous and as there is only a single commodity, it should be clear that only a different distribution of output between the younger agents and the elderly perhaps renders such an improvement possible. We may therefore introduce a sequence (b_t) of transfers or benefits which will be referred to as a *transfer-scheme*. In every period t, some portion b_t of national income is taken from the younger and given to the elderly if $b_t > 0$, and vice versa if $b_t < 0$. If no generation shall be made worse off, every feasible transfer scheme must have three specific properties which are listed below:

$$b_1 \geq 0, \tag{73}$$

$$b_t \geq R_t \cdot b_{t-1} \quad \text{for all } t \geq 2, \tag{74}$$

$$b_t \leq Y_t \equiv G_t \cdot Y_{t-1} \quad \text{for all } t \geq 2. \tag{75}$$

The first condition states that a non-negative amount must be given to the older agents alive at the inception of time if these are not to be made worse off. The reason is that they are already dead in the following period and cannot be compensated. This is different with the younger agents who may be taxed in period t if they are properly compensated one period ahead. The meaning of "properly" is delineated in (74): If b_t is taken away from an agent in period t-1, the latter must be given at least $R_t \cdot b_t$ one period later because he has been free to exchange present for future consumption at the rate R_t. Thus, $b_t < R_t \cdot b_{t-1}$ would either make the agent worse off or would contradict the utility maximization hypothesis. — The last property of a Pareto-improving transfer scheme is a feasibility condition which requires the transfer in period t not to exceed national income Y_t. National income, in turn, equals G_t times Y_{t-1} by virtue of our definition of a real growth factor. Simple recursions of (74) and (75) yield the following relationships:

$$b_t \geq b_1 \cdot \prod_{\tau=2}^{t} R_\tau . \tag{74'}$$

$$b_t \leq Y_1 \cdot \prod_{\tau=2}^{t} G_\tau . \tag{75'}$$

That is to say, the size of Pareto-improving transfers *must grow at least at the rate of interest* (74') and *may not grow faster than national income* (75'). Combining these two inequalities and rearranging terms we obtain a characterization of Pareto-improving transfer schemes:

$$\prod_{\tau=2}^{t} \frac{G_\tau}{R_\tau} \geq \frac{b_1}{Y_1} . \tag{76}$$

Now suppose that the compound interest rate eventually exceeds the compound growth rate, i.e.

$$\liminf_{t \to \infty} \prod_{\tau=2}^{t} \frac{G_\tau}{R_\tau} = 0. \tag{77}$$

If the ratio of compound growth and interest rates is not bounded away from zero, the right-hand side in (76) must vanish, too. As Y_1 is a given positive number, this implies $b_1 = 0$: there exists no Pareto-improving transfer scheme, and the original allocation is dynamically efficient. Of course, condition (77) is a special case of (28) from chapter 3 for a one-commodity world.

The perhaps best illustration of this result is *government debt* in a Diamond (1965) model. Assume that a payment $b_1>0$ out of the general budget is made to the elderly. The payment is not financed via taxation, as this would hurt the younger agents. Instead, the government incurs a debt $D=b_1$. If, by the same token, none of the future generations shall be required to repay that debt, D will grow at the rate of interest. This is the meaning of equations (74) and (74'). The government bonds issued are bought by the younger agents who have an income $w_t \leq Y_t$ in the Diamond model. Hence, D may not grow faster than Y_t, as stated in (75) and (75').

Now, if (77) holds, it turns out to be impossible to meet these two requirements simultaneously and permanently because the interest rate exceeds the growth rate in the long run. Therefore, eventually some generation must be taxed, and then $b_1>0$ is not a Pareto-improvement but only a *redistribution* of welfare between generations. The original allocation is thus dynamically efficient. This result follows from a sort of backward induction: Condition (77) forces the size of transfers relative to national income (b_t/Y_t) to vanish in the far future; but then they must also vanish at present if no one shall be made worse off.

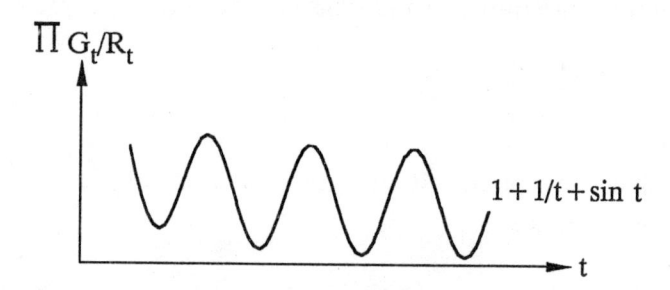

$\prod G_t/R_t$

$1+1/t+\sin t$

Figure 1

From this reasoning it is easily inferred why all of our efficiency conditions refer to the *limit infimum*: The ratio of compound growth and interest rates need not converge to zero; it suffices that the sequence repeatedly approaches zero in the far future and then, maybe, becomes strictly positive again. For example, consider the path $1+1/t+\sin t$, as depicted in figure 1. Its limit infimum equals zero so that the associated equilibrium must be dynamically efficient. For a path as $1.1 + 1/t + \sin t$, this would not necessarily be true.

To summarize. In the present section the issue of dynamic efficiency has been analyzed within a simple model of economic growth which performed well in bringing out the central idea behind the abstract propositions from chapters 2 to 5: Dynamic inefficiency occurs when it is possible to redistribute income from the young to the old — not the other way round. Once such a redistribution has been initiated, it must continue forever if no one is to be made worse off; but it *cannot* continue forever when the compound interest rate eventually exceeds the compound growth rate. This is because the transfers must at least grow at the rate of interest and can at most grow at the rate of growth. The scope of the model presented here, however, is narrow especially since income has been assumed to be exogenous. This has been done because otherwise the introduction of a transfer scheme could possibly *increase* national income. As a consequence, nothing about dynamic efficiency could be said via a look at the original interest and growth rates. At this stage the far more powerful results from chapter 2 come into play which show such degenerate behaviour to be impossible if the original state is a competitive equilibrium.

6.2 A Simple Economy with Land

An important claim of our theoretical study has been that the mere existence of a nonproducible productive factor, i.e. land, prevents an economy from accumulating "too much" — provided that land does not eventually drop out of the model. However, the analysis conducted so far did not properly reveal the workings of this automatic adjustment mechanism which effectively renders every competitive growth path Pareto-efficient. We now want to proffer a simple macroeconomic model with land as a factor of production.

The model is perfectly analogous to Diamond's (1965) neoclassical growth model except that labour and land instead of labour and real

Chapter 6. Examples and Applications

capital are the two factors of production. The following draws heavily on my (1991) paper, and when writing it in 1989 I was unaware of another contribution to the issue of dynamic efficiency in a model with endogenous rent formation. But McCallum (1987), in a volume on monetary economics, has advanced a similar argument before, restricted to steady state growth paths[1]. He has also conjectured that, in a framework with a fixed factor of production, the steady state assumption comes close to assuming all production and utility functions to be Cobb-Douglas. This is right, and precisely *because* it is right, the analysis of chapter 4 has been concerned with non-steady state growth paths.

Our model consists of a representative household and a representative firm. In every period, the *firm* solves

$$\max_{(N_t, L_t) \geq 0} \pi_t = Y_t - w_t \cdot N_t - \varrho_t \cdot L_t \qquad (78)$$

$$\text{s.t.} \quad Y_t = N_t^{1-\alpha} \cdot L^\alpha, \qquad 0 < \alpha < 1,$$

where π are profits, Y is national income or output ("corn"), N labour input, w the real wage rate and F a Cobb-Douglas production function. L denotes acres of land, written l_t on a per-capita base ($l_t := L/N_t$), ϱ represents the rent, measured in pounds of corn per acre and per year, and q is the *spot* price of land, measured in pounds of corn per acre. National income splits up into wage income ($w \cdot N$) and rent income ($\varrho \cdot L$) whereas profits vanish by virtue of constant returns to scale. Observe that (78) is a *static* maximization problem as all time indices refer to period t. Because L is constant over time, the equilibrium values of the wage and the rents are given by the marginal productivity conditions

$$w_t = (1-\alpha) \cdot l_t^\alpha \ ; \qquad \varrho_t = \alpha \cdot l_t^{\alpha-1} \qquad (79)$$

and only depend on the labour force N_t born in period t. As population is also supposed to be exogenous, the paths of the real wage rate (w_t) and the rent (ϱ_t) are independent of the households' decisions. This

---

1 By contrast, the Homburg (1991) paper deals with arbitrary growth paths and employs the efficiency criterion (77). McCallum's paper was brought to my mind by Bruno Schönfelder, when I presented the paper at Munich University in 1989.

simplifies the model considerably. The representative *household* lives for two periods and solves

$$\max_{(c_t^1, c_{t+1}^2, l_t) \geq 0} U = (c_t^1)^\beta \cdot (c_{t+1}^2)^{1-\beta}, \quad 0 \leq \beta < 1, \tag{80}$$

s.t. (i) $c_t^1 + q_t \cdot l_t = w_t$,

(ii) $c_{t+1}^2 = (q_{t+1} + \varrho_{t+1}) \cdot l_t$,

where, as usual, c_t^1 denotes consumption when young and c_{t+1}^2 consumption when old. Before interpreting these two budget constraints recall what happens in the Diamond model where people save via accumulation of real capital.

Diamond model: Subject to $c_t^1 + s_t = w_t$, the younger agents buy capital goods at the price $p_t \equiv 1$ (this price directly follows from the assumption of a one-sector economy). They lease the capital goods to the firms, obtaining an interest r_{t+1} in return, and eventually sell them at the ruling price $p_{t+1} \equiv 1$. Thus the budget constraint of the elderly reads $c_{t+1}^2 = (1 + r_{t+1}) \cdot s_t$. The *interest factor* can be calculated as $R_{t+1} := (p_{t+1} + r_{t+1})/p_t$ or simply as $1 + r_{t+1}$.

Model with land: Here people can buy land during the first period of their lives in order to provide for their old age. Consumption when young plus land purchases ($q_t \cdot l_t$) exhaust the wage income. Later on, an agent will lease the land to a firm in exchange for the rent ϱ_{t+1} and finally will dispose of the land at the price q_{t+1}. Thus the *interest factor* becomes

$$R_{t+1} := \frac{q_{t+1} + \varrho_{t+1}}{q_t}. \tag{81}$$

As an example, R_{t+1} just equals $1 + \varrho_{t+1}$ when the land's spot price remains constant. But there is no reason why this price should remain constant — and if not, R_{t+1} will either exceed or fall short of $1 + \varrho_{t+1}$. A potential real estate investor habitually compares the variable R_{t+1} thus defined with the return on real capital, knowing that a considerable part of the return on land consists of the increase in the land's price over time. It is precisely for this reason that the direct return on land, i.e. the expression ϱ_{t+1}/q_t, is normally smaller than the interest on safe assets.

Chapter 6. Examples and Applications

In both the Diamond model and the model with land the old agents, N_{t-1} in number, only spend their savings and thus act purely passively whereas the younger agents influence the interest rate via their savings decisions. We thus recognize the supply of land to be perfectly inelastic with respect to the price q_t: the elderly are willing to sell their land at any non-negative price. Therefore, free disposal of land implies

$$q_t \geq 0 \quad \text{for all t.} \tag{82}$$

For the younger agents, the decision-making process is a bit more involved than in the Diamond model since the return on land depends on its future price q_{t+1} (as well as on ϱ_{t+1}). But owing to the Cobb-Douglas utility function, the younger agents' demand for land simply obeys

$$l_t^d = (1-\beta) \cdot w_t / q_t \tag{83}$$

and is thus independent of the land's future price. The reason is, of course, that this particular utility function generates interest inelastic "savings". Assuming the labour market and the market for land services to clear, the model boils down to a single equilibrium condition with q_t as the endogenous variable, whereas w_t and ϱ_t are exogenously given:

$$L_t^d \stackrel{!}{=} L \iff l_t^d \stackrel{!}{=} l_t \iff (1-\beta) \cdot w_t / q_t \stackrel{!}{=} l_t \ . \tag{84}$$

Substituting wages from (79) into (84) and solving for q_t shows the land's price to be a decreasing function of the land/labour ratio:

$$q_t = (1-\alpha) \cdot (1-\beta) \cdot l_t^{\alpha-1} \ . \tag{85}$$

And finally, inserting this value of q_t together with ϱ_t from (79) into (81), the equilibrium value of the interest factor is seen to equal

$$R_{t+1} = [1 + \frac{\alpha}{(1-\alpha)(1-\beta)}] \cdot (l_t / l_{t+1})^{1-\alpha}. \tag{86}$$

This equation yields an important result when we follow Diamond in concentrating on steady states, assuming population to grow at a constant rate $n > -1$. Population at time t is now given by $N_t = (1+n)^t$ which, in turn, implies $l_t = (1+n)^{-t}$: The land/labour ratio $l_t = L/N_t$ permanently decreases in an economy with positive population growth. Because, in equation (86), l_t/l_{t+1} now simply equals $1+n$, the *steady state interest factor* becomes

$$R = [1 + \frac{\alpha}{(1-\alpha)(1-\beta)}] \cdot (1+n)^{1-\alpha}, \qquad (87)$$

whereas the *steady state growth factor* equals[1])

$$G := \frac{Y_{t+1}}{Y_t} = (1+n)^{1-\alpha}. \qquad (88)$$

Comparing these two expressions we immediately see that *the interest factor strictly exceeds the growth factor* for all admissible values of the parameters α, β, and n. Therefore, steady state growth in our simple economy with land is necessarily *Pareto-optimal*, as can be inferred from (77). Moreover, the growth path cannot obey the *Golden Rule* of accumulation, R and G cannot coincide.

The intuition behind this result is as follows. With a Cobb-Douglas utility function (which is homothetic), the demand for future consumption (c^2) and consequently the demand for land ($q \cdot L$) will grow at the rate G-1, irrespective of the behaviour of the interest factor. As L is fixed, however, the increasing demand for land will only bid up its *price*. We can therefore conclude that q_{t+1}/q_t, the growth of the land's price, equals the growth of national income. But the interest factor R is q_{t+1}/q_t *plus* ϱ_{t+1}/q_t, where ϱ_{t+1}/q_t is a strictly positive number. Hence, the interest factor will be in excess of the growth factor. The existence of land thus rules out inefficient as well as Golden Rule growth paths.

Let us try to generalize this result informally, increasing the vividness of the exposition of this adjustment mechanism. In what follows we only assume the rent to be a constant fraction of national income, which is to say that the *land's income share* $\lambda := \varrho \cdot L/Y$ remains unchanged. Now consider again the interest factor, reproduced here for convenience.

---

1 In Diamond's model the growth factor is simply 1+n: output, capital and population grow at a common constant rate. This is different in our model with land since only one factor of production (the labour force) is allowed to increase. The equality (88) directly follows from the production function (78) because (1-α) is the partial elasticity of output with respect to labour.

$$R_{t+1} := \frac{q_{t+1} + \varrho_{t+1}}{q_t}. \tag{81}$$

Regarding the land's spot price, there are three possible cases:

- First, q_t may grow at the same rate as national income Y_t. Then, the interest factor will obviously exceed the growth factor G_t as it equals G_t *plus* a strictly positive number, viz. ϱ_{t+1}/q_t.

- Second, q_t may grow faster than national income. In this case, R_t will exceed G_t all the more.

- And third, q_t may grow less fast than national income. Then, the ratio ϱ_{t+1}/q_t and thus R_{t+1} itself even approaches infinity because the rent grows at the rate G_t.

Empirically, the first of the above cases seems to be a good approximation of what happens in the real world; I want to offer but two examples. In his valuable book "One Hundred Years of Land Values in Chicago", Hoyt (1933) has traced "The Relation between the Growth of Chicago and the Rise of its Land Values". He found both population and land values to have risen from 1835: 1 to 1933: 700, i.e. by some 70,000%[1]. In Hoyt's figure 76, the growth of land values amazingly parallels the increase in population. Our second example refers to the Federal Republic of Germany and the time span 1971 to 1989. During that period, land values for single-family houses rose by 188% whereas nominal GDP rose by 198%[2]. This is only casual observation, of course, but empirical studies concerning the relationship between national income and land prices are rare[3].

---

[1] Admittedly, population has not been the sole source of economic growth during the period 1835 to 1933, and there has been some inflation. But taking these additional factors into account does not change the result substantially, as can be inferred from Hoyt's figures 76 and 77.

[2] Sources: Sachverständigenrat (1990) for gross domestic product; own calculations for land values. The latter are based on data from the federation of German real estate brokers (Ring Deutscher Makler, RDM) which were published since 1971. The above number is an index of land values in 30 major German cities.

[3] The only exception I know of is Rhee (1991) whose figures suggest that in the US, the land's income share has declined until the 1950's and thereafter has remained more or less constant.

Let us try to give yet another interpretation of how land prevents an economy from accumulating "too much". The latter phenomenon is known to occur when the agents *overrate* future consumption: Here, individuals perceive to built up stocks of storable commodities for future consumption – whilst society as a whole will never actually consume that stock but will push it into the indefinite future. The resulting resource allocation can possibly be improved upon by means of a Samuelson (1958) type "social contract" which distributes income from the young to the old and which, from the individual's perspective, acts as savings whereas it is not savings from an aggregate viewpoint because no goods are actually stored.

Now, the same holds true for land: Land facilitates transferring *value* into the future without requiring to build up *commodity stocks*. Consider an initially efficient state and ask what happens if all agents suddenly want to save more: A capital economy, like Diamond's, will then be apt to accumulate too vast a capital stock in order to meet this desire for greater savings. In an economy with land, by contrast, only the land's *price* will rise and bring about an increase in the value of savings. No consumption of physical goods has to be postponed actually. Quite on the contrary, aggregate consumption may *rise* because the older land owners can now afford more consumption after selling their real estate. This is an automatic adjustment mechanism which precludes overaccumulation.

What about a model with land *and* real capital, the reader may ask. It is easy to see that such an economy will essentially work like an economy with land only: An investor, when considering to buy either real capital or land, will naturally compare the respective yields of these assets. As the return on land cannot fall short of or equal the growth rate, real capital must also yield a return in excess of the growth rate. If not, investors would reduce the capital stock and buy land instead, thereby pushing up consumption via the afore-mentioned adjustment mechanism. This even holds when the value of real capital is very large as compared to the value of land.

I do not know whether the above informal reasoning is entirely convincing – proofs for more general economies can be found in chapter 4.

6.3 Turgot's Theory of Fructification

The beginning of economics has also been the beginning of interest theory. The latter branch, as has often been observed, is basically concerned with a single problem only. It is why interest rates are, or should be, positive. This is so intriguing a question because, as Homer (1963) reports, interest has been positive over several thousand years – since Babylon. The theoretical explanation of this phenomenon, however, is less than obvious; after all, interest is the relative price of future to present goods, and there exists no *a priori* presumption of why present goods should have always been dearer. A more precise version of the above question reads whether or not interest will be strictly positive in a *stationary state*, i.e. along a path were the economy replicates from period to period.

The first serious attack at the problem under consideration was made by Jacques Turgot, the former minister of finance under Louis XVI. Turgot's theory of interest, though developed as early as 1766, did by no means play an important rôle in the writings of the classical economists; it was critized and given the name "theory of fructification" by Böhm-Bawerk at the turn of the century, and then, by and large, fell into oblivion again. In this section I want to argue that Turgot's approach to explaining interest is not only the first but also perhaps the best one. What I mean by a "good" theory of interest will be made clear at the end of the section when the theory of fructification will be compared with neoclassical and neo-austrian approaches. Let us delineate Turgot's approach first.

Turgot was something like a "para-physiocrat": he did not adhere strictly to the edifice set forth by François Quesnay and his followers, but the notion of the productiveness of nature obviously formed his thinking. It is no accident, then, that the main ingredient of Turgot's interest theory is the existence of productive land. In section 57 of his *Réflexions*, Turgot introduced the concept of a *denier du prix de terres* which we shall call *denier* for short. Considering a particular real estate, the *denier* is simply the ratio of the land's price and its annual rent. Thus,

$$\textit{Denier du prix de terres:} \quad d := \frac{q}{\varrho}. \tag{89}$$

where q and ϱ represent the stationary values of the price and the rent, respectively. Obviously, the *denier* simply equals the inverse of the interest rate. In section 89, Turgot argues as follows:

"Clearly, the value of real estate is the higher the lower is the interest rate. A man who is entitled to a rent of 50,000 Livres holds a property of but 1 million if selling his real estate at a *denier* of 20 [the interest rate being 5%]; but he possesses 2 millions if selling his estate at a *denier* of 40 [the interest rate being 2 1/2%]."

Now, we only need to go a single step further and supplement: "If the interest rate approached zero, the *denier* would become infinite." Because, in stationary equilibrium, land has certainly a finite value, such is impossible and the interest rate must be strictly positive.

Turgot also recognized that the interplay of the *denier* and the interest rate preclude any investment whose return falls short of the return on land; though, of course, he did not know this to be a good thing because the danger of dynamic inefficiency was only discovered some 200 years later. Let us denote the return on real capital by r and the interest factor by R := 1 + r. Then, due to arbitrage[1],

$$1+r = R = \frac{q+\varrho}{q} \Leftrightarrow r = \frac{1}{d}. \tag{90}$$

As the *denier* is a real number like 20 or 50, capital must yield a strictly positive return or the investment will not be undertaken. Hence, *every stationary state of an economy with land is dynamically efficient*. For, the growth rate equals zero, the interest rate strictly exceeds the growth rate, and thus condition (77) is fulfilled. Returning to theorem 3 for a moment, we see that this result extends to almost arbitrarily general economies: In section 4.5 it was proven that economies with land display efficient economic growth when the land's income share is bounded away from zero; cf. equation (54). Now, this prerequirement is *automatically* met in a stationary state since the very definition of such a state entails

---

1 Turgot's own argument is a bit more subtle: He states, in sections 86 and 87, that the yield of real capital invested in trade or manufacturing must exceed the interest paid on bonds which, in turn, must exceed the return on land. This is because land is the safest asset and real capital the most insecure.

a constant income share of land. A positive constant income share is plainly bounded away from zero, so the interest rate must be strictly positive and the allocation is Pareto-optimal.

Summing up thus far, we have seen that Turgot's theory of fructification yields a perfect explanation of why interest will be strictly positive in stationary equilibrium. Many economists of our century − who have hotly debated this issue[1] − arrived at a different conclusion. Pigou for instance, when writing an entire volume on *The Economics of Stationary States*, passed the following judgement:

"This conclusion, it will be noticed, runs counter to the opinion, which has sometimes been entertained, that in a stationary state the rate of interest must necessarily be nil. That opinion has been vigorously sponsored by Professor Schumpeter. It also appears to have been held by Wicksell. For he writes: 'If we consider society as a whole, and regard the average economic conditions as *approximately* stationary, the progressive accumulation of capital must be regarded as economic so long as any rate of interest, however low, exists. Under such conditions we should expect the continued accumulation of capital − though at a diminishing rate − and at the same time a continued fall in the rate of interest.'

This implies that a completely stationary state, with its stock of capital constant, is only possible provided that the rate of interest is nil. In the light of the foregoing argument it seems plain that this view is incorrect. It is necessary to a stationary state that the capital stock shall stand at such a level that the rate of interest is equal to Robinson's rate of discounting future satisfactions. If that rate is nil, then the rate of interest must also be nil. But that rate need not be nil. So far as *a priori* considerations go, it may be anything whatever, 50 per cent per annum or even *minus* 50 per cent per annum. What it is in actuality is brute fact depending on Robinson's mental make-up. For a representative Englishman of the present day it is probably positive and fairly small."[2]

---

1 Good expositions of this discussion can be found in Kuenne (1963) or Faber (1979). The principal opponents were Böhm-Bawerk (1913) on the one side and Schumpeter (1913) on the other. The latter attributed interest entirely to growth and maintained that the interest rate would vanish in stationary equilibrium. The former thought the interest rate would be positive, owing to the second and third of his famous "reasons" for interest, viz. time preference and capital productivity.

2 Pigou (1935; 54f; italics in original). Pigou is referring to Wicksell (1934).

Pigou's view is obviously correct when applied to economies of the Samuelson (1958) or Diamond (1965) type; but incorrect once the existence of land is taken into account. Turgot's theory of fructification yields a definite solution to the afore-mentioned debate about the sign of the interest rate in stationary equilibrium: Schumpeter and Wicksell are wrong whereas Böhm-Bawerk (and Knight) are right for the wrong reasons; and Keynes' prediction of an "euthanasia of the rentier" turns out to be a myth. It seems to me that the whole debate has been somewhat misplaced since none of the participants would have deliberately denied the importance of land; and it is all the more astonishing that Schumpeter, the greatest historian among economic theorists, was perfectly aware of Turgot's writings and had even ranked him above Adam Smith — yet did not make use of Turgot's theory of fructification.

Contemporary authors have rarely taken up Turgot's reasoning — if at all, then in footnotes or remarks. The argument familiar today runs as follows: In a *steady state* where some *exogenous rent* grows at the common rate g, the interest rate r cannot be smaller than g if the rent is to have a finite present value. Such statements can be found, for instance, in Malinvaud (1953; 257), Niehans (1966), Tirole (1985; 1079), or Muller and Woodford (1988; 262). It was perhaps the combination of *steady state* and *exogenous rent*-assumptions which has induced readers — as well as the authors themselves — to be sceptical about the relevance of such a line of reasoning: We have already indicated that these two premises can be reconciled in special cases only. The analysis of chapter 4, however, should have made plain that these very assumptions are superfluous. Therefore I think the theory of fructification should be given a more important rôle in modern growth theory.

This brings me to the final point I want to make in the present section. I wish to argue that the theory of fructification is superior to alternative approaches in the sense that it does not rely on *ad hoc* assumptions. Consider the following three premises:

(A)   Land is either useful or productive.
(B.1) Capital (or roundabout production) is productive.
(B.2) Future utilities are discounted.

I consider these to be equally "good" assumptions. The theory of fructification rests on (A) whereas both neoclassical and neo-Austrian theories rely on (B). From (A) it directly follows that the interest rate is strictly positive in a stationary economy; and this result directly extends to economies with positive growth rates. Moreover, interest will be strictly positive regardless of what we assume about time preference or production possibilities. This is a direct implication of corollary 3 on interest, growth and dynamic efficiency (cf. section 3.3) in conjunction with theorem 3 on land and dynamic efficiency (cf. section 4.5). In the derivation of these propositions, no special behavioural assumptions have been employed.

Now, what can be inferred from (B)? The answer, as is well known, reads: nothing. We can build stationary economies where more capital facilitates more future production and where households prefer present to future consumption and where interest is negative nevertheless. Think of Samuelson's (1958) consumption-loan model, for instance. Without a "social contract", interest rates come to -100% whatever is assumed about time preference. The reason is that households only obtain endowments during the first periods of their lives and hence desperately try to transform present into future consumption even if the latter is valued less high. Regarding capital, we may well assume that any increase in capital input today allows having more output tomorrow. Yet, such does not imply positive interest because positive interest additionally requires that the increase in output more than counterbalances capital depreciation.

Therefore, assumptions (B) do not themselves imply the existence of positive interest, and additional (*ad hoc*) premises have to be made, of the kind that capital is productive "enough" etc. But this comes close to implicit reasoning. For sure, I do not offend the idea that "capital productivity" or "time preference" tend to raise interest but only want to point out that these facts are neither necessary nor sufficient to establish positive interest. Assumption (A), on the other hand, at least explains why interest rates have always been positive in the past. The reason simply is that the land's income share did not sharply decline — though it did also not rise permanently, as Ricardo conjectured in his most famous prediction.

6.4 A Capital Reserve System without Capital

In modern societies provisions for old age take either of the following forms. For one, people can accumulate assets during the working period and then live on the wealth plus interest when old. Or, the state may set up a public pension scheme such that the elderly are directly supported by the young and no capital will be accumulated. The first system is usually referred to as a *capital reserve system* (CR) whilst the second has been termed *pay-as-you-go system* (PAYG). Starting not only with some influential papers by Martin Feldstein there has been an ongoing concern about which of the two systems should be preferred; and no agreement has been reached as yet. Here are two of the basic arguments:

- The adherants to CR, among them Feldstein (1977b), suspect PAYG to depress national savings, which is indeed true under rather plausible premises. And they say that only CR allows to build up a "buffer stock" yielding real interest, which is a good thing especially when population shrinks. In sum, PAYG is inefficient and especially liable to changes in population.

- Opponents of this view, like Lerner (1959), Mackenroth (1952) or Meinhold (1985), doubt that society as a whole can secure itself against population changes by means of capital accumulation. They often believe aggregate savings to be a "financial illusion": With an aging population the supply on the asset market will by far exceed the demand, and the assets' *values* will sharply decline. Thus, the argument in favour of CR is considered to be a fallacy of composition, and PAYG is preferred.

In what follows I will construct a model which in a sense unifies the above views and shows them to be not mutually exclusive. I analyze a capital reserve system *without* real capital where people save only via the acquisition of land. This is a relevant, though extreme, assumption for several reasons: Land makes up a very considerable part of national wealth and is often used as a provision for old age. In most countries, moreover, banks and insurance companies are forced by the law to hold some minimum fraction of their wealth in form of real estate or equally secure assets; they cannot simply invest abroad when interest rates at home become unfavourable.

The model I use is basically identical to the simple economy with land introduced in section 6.2 and will not be explained again in detail. Young households buy land – denoted by l_t on a per capita base – at the price q_t, lease it to the firms in exchange for a rent payment ϱ_{t+1}, and finally sell the land at the price q_{t+1}. With a Cobb-Douglas utility function, the households' maximization problem reads:

$$\max_{(c_t^1, c_{t+1}^2, l_t) \geq 0} U = (c_t^1)^\beta \cdot (c_{t+1}^2)^{1-\beta}, \quad 0 \leq \beta < 1, \tag{91}$$

s.t. (i) $c_t^1 + q_t \cdot l_t = w_t$,

(ii) $c_{t+1}^2 = (q_{t+1} + \varrho_{t+1}) \cdot l_t$.

By solving (91) we obtain the optimal quantities

$$c_t^1 = \beta \cdot w_t; \quad c_{t+1}^2 = (1-\beta) \cdot R_{t+1} \cdot w_t; \quad l_t^d = (1-\beta) \cdot w_t / q_t, \tag{92}$$

where R_{t+1} again denotes the interest factor

$$R_{t+1} := \frac{q_{t+1} + \varrho_{t+1}}{q_t}. \tag{93}$$

The firm, producing output, Y, by means of labour input, N, and land, L, maximizes total profits in every period:

$$\max_{(N_t, L_t) \geq 0} \pi_t = Y_t - w_t \cdot N_t - \varrho_t \cdot L_t \tag{94}$$

s.t. $Y_t = N_t^{1-\alpha} \cdot L^\alpha, \quad 0 < \alpha < 1,$

from which the equilibrium values of the wage rate and the rent can directly be inferred:

$$w_t = (1-\alpha) \cdot l_t^\alpha; \quad \varrho_t = \alpha \cdot l_t^{\alpha-1}. \tag{95}$$

The issue of payments to the elderly gains attention precisely if population changes, i.e. if the economy is *not* in a steady state. We therefore want to consider arbitrary growth paths, defining the *rate of population growth* in period t by $1+n_{t+1} := N_{t+1}/N_t$. In this case, the quantity of land per capita (L/N) obeys $l_t/l_{t+1} = 1+n_{t+1}$: it decreases whenever population grows and increases whenever population declines. Substituting this into the definition of the interest factor (86) yields:

$$R_{t+1} = [1 + \frac{\alpha}{(1-\alpha)(1-\beta)}] \cdot (1+n_{t+1})^{1-\alpha}. \tag{96}$$

Hence, the participants of a capital reserve system without real capital obtain a strictly positive return on their contributions when population grows or at least remains constant; in these cases, $R_{t+1} > 1$. Before commenting on this further, let us introduce a pay-as-you-go system where every young man must contribute a constant fraction τ of his wage income when young and obtains a pension payment p_{t+1} when old. It is well-known from Samuelson (1958) and Aaron (1966) that the *implicit rate of return* (denoted by i) of PAYG simply equals the growth rate of total wage income:

$$1 + i_{t+1} := \frac{w_{t+1} \cdot N_{t+1}}{w_t \cdot N_t} = (1+n_{t+1})^{1-\alpha}. \tag{97}$$

The right-hand side of (97) has been calculated by substituting $l_t/l_{t+1} = 1 + n_{t+1}$ into (95). Let us finally combine (86) and (97) in order to compare CR and PAYG:

$$R_{t+1} = [1 + \frac{\alpha}{(1-\alpha)(1-\beta)}] \cdot (1+i_{t+1}). \tag{98}$$

In equation (98), we recognize the return on contributions to CR on the left and the return on PAYG on the right. These two are seen to obey a strict relationship which depends only on the parameters α and β, and the relationship is such that

- the return of CR strictly exceeds the return of PAYG, irrespective of the growth rate;

- the elasticity of the interest factor with respect to $1+i$ equals unity.

What is the intuition behind these results? Suppose that labour's income share α equals 0.5 and that population in period $t+1$ is four times as high as population in period t. Then, as can be inferred from (97), aggregate wage income doubles from period to period. The return of PAYG equals 100% because, with a constant contribution rate τ, every generation will pay twice the amount the preceding generation has paid one period before. The price of land, however, due to the land's scarcity and the constant savings ratio, will double also. And as savings in form of land yield a rent payment in addition, the total return of CR must strictly exceed that of PAYG. This explains why any young individual, if asked, will prefer CR to PAYG.

Assume now that population growth suddenly falls to 0% per period. As a consequence, every generation contributes the same amount to PAYG, so the return on these contributions becomes zero. Participants of CR will no longer profit from an increasing price of land and will thus be hurt, too; yet they continue to obtain the rent, which implies a strictly positive return on contributions to CR. From the above statement concerning the elasticities we see that the members of the two systems are equally hurt by reductions in the growth rate. However, the members of CR are always better off.

This simple model sheds some new light on a number of interesting questions. For one, many authors have argued that a market economy is in need of either a "social contract" or money as a store of value because else it could become difficult to transfer wealth between generations. Our own view is similar to Tobin's (1980; 84) who once expressed his doubts on monetary overlapping-generations models thus: "[I]f a nonreproducible asset has been needed for intergenerational transfers of wealth, land has always been available. Quantitatively it has been a much more important store of value than money."

A closely related issue concerns a popular argument which is often brought forward against capital reserve systems and which runs as follows: Establishing a capital reserve system would entail such vast capital stocks — by far higher than the ones already existing in our economies — that the marginal productivity of capital were liable to become negative. Such a view is demonstrably invalid. One only has to recognize that the transfer of *value* between generations does not imply a transfer of *physical goods* — it suffices perfectly if the *price* of some nonproducible asset rises. And the price of land certainly *will* rise in a growing economy whenever the marginal productivity of capital tends to become negative. This follows simply from arbitrage.

Let us finally comment on a stimulating model by Merton (1983) who considers PAYG as some kind of insurance. In a portfolio-theoretic framework, Merton argues that risk-averse households will wish to take part in *both* CR and PAYG if the respective yields of these two systems are uncertain. In Merton's framework interest and growth factors are stochastic variables which can in principle assume any value; and a man fearing that the growth rate may exceed the interest rate in the future may wish to insure himself against this risk via a contribution to PAYG, even if the latter's expected return were smaller.

Our above model supports a different view which, I must warn, is not air-tight: Considering population growth as a stochastic variable, both R_t and $1+i_t$ will follow a stochastic process – but obviously first-order stochastic dominance prevails, as can be seen from (96): The return of CR will always exceed that of PAYG, and no one will wish to take part in PAYG even in this uncertain world.

Admittedly, this extreme result (first-order stochastic dominance) is due to the constant savings ratio which implies a strict proportionality between the land's price and aggregate wage income; cf. (92). But I believe there is some truth in this model because it is only too plausible that elder house-owners, for instance, directly profit from unexpected increases in the income of the young. Anyway, our whole analysis suggests that it would be misleading to consider interest and growth rates as independent stochastic processes.

In this section we have compared a capital reserve system with a pay-as-you-go system, the former having the peculiar feature that no real capital but only land is used as a store of value. Among our main findings were that (i) CR will generally be preferred to PAYG by younger individuals, (ii) increases in the land's price perfectly suffice to transfer arbitrarily large amounts of wealth between generations, (iii) the return of CR is equally liable to changes in the growth rate as is the return of PAYG. It should be clear that most of these result, in one form or another, extend to more realistic capital reserve systems where both land and real capital are used as stores of value. This is simply because the introduction of physical capital, due to arbitrage, cannot make savers worse off.

6.5 Old Masters and Bubbles

One of our main themes has been that the presence of land will rule out dynamically inefficient growth paths. But it was already in chapter 4 that we suggested to interpret the term "land" not too literally — land in our analytical sense simply means a productive or useful commodity which is durable and cannot be reproduced. The existence of a wide variety of such goods has been acknowledged for long. Ricardo (1817; 6; italics added), for instance, just when beginning to set forth his labour theory of value, writes:

> "There are some commodities, the value of which is determined by their scarcity alone. No labour can increase the quantity of such goods, and therefore their value cannot be lowered by an increased supply. Some rare statues and pictures, scarce books and coins, wines of a peculiar quality, which can be made only from grapes grown on a particular soil, of which there is a very limited quantity, are all of this description. Their value is wholly independent of the quantity of labour originally necessary to produce them, *and varies with the varying wealth and inclinations of those who are desirous to possess them.*"

We now want to show by means of an example that the presence of such goods rules out dynamic inefficiency once these "inclinations" obey some mild regularity assumption. The following analysis thus complements sections 6.2 and 6.4 in that we will concentrate on useful as opposed to productive "land". During the rest of this section, "land" may either be interpreted as some item from Ricardo's list or, empirically perhaps more importantly, as a household's demand for housing.

The idea behind our partial equilibrium model is this one: A representative household's savings can principally take either of two forms: First, the household can acquire a perfectly useless asset in the capital market, obtaining an interest payment thereon. Second, it may buy a useful durable good such as a valuable picture — an Old Master, as we may call it — or a house to live in. An Old Master — costing q_t when the household is young and q_{t+1} when it is old — not only yields a monetary return q_{t+1}/q_t but also direct utility. Assuming the utility function to be Cobb-Douglas, with positive parameters $\alpha, \beta, \gamma < 1$ such that $\alpha + \beta + \gamma = 1$, the representative household's decision problem reads:

6.5 Old Masters and Bubbles

$$\max_{(c_t^1, c_{t+1}^2, s_t, l_t) \geq 0} U = (c_t^1)^\alpha \cdot (c_{t+1}^2)^\beta \cdot (l_t)^\gamma, \qquad (99)$$

s.t. (i) $c_t^1 + s_t + q_t \cdot l_t = w_t$,

(ii) $c_{t+1}^2 = R_{t+1} \cdot s_t + q_{t+1} \cdot l_t$.

Here w, R, c, s represent wages, interest, consumption (when young and when old) and savings, respectively. The symbol l_t denotes the quantity of Old Masters (or housing) a young household demands. This quantity has been put into the utility function, and (ii) shows that the Old Master will be sold one period ahead. Its market price is q_t in period t and q_{t+1} in period t+1. Therefore, when wishing to buy a single unit of the Old Master, the household's other consumption need not be reduced by q_t but only by $q_t - q_{t+1}/R_{t+1}$; this latter value may be called the Old Master's *shadow rent*.

Models like the present one must be tackled with some care because the shadow rent depends on three variables, and the equilibrium conditions – as is well known – will not generally suffice to determine them uniquely, or at least locally uniquely. We are referring here to the famous *indeterminacy* which has first been pointed out by Calvo (1978) in a very similar framework. Indeterminacy means that there exists a continuum of equilibria; and such an occurence is annoying because it precludes meaningful comparative statics. Regarding *efficiency* analysis, however, indeterminacy will not bother us, as will become clear in a moment: There may well exist a continuum of equilibria, yet all of them will turn out to be efficient.

In order to demonstrate that, let us complete our model by assuming wage rates, interest rates, and population to be given by arbitrary positive sequences. In particular, N_t representing the number of households born at time t, we will use capital letters $W_t := w_t \cdot N_t$ and $L := l_t \cdot N_t$ to denote aggregate variables. Forming a Lagrangean from (99) and applying the standard algorithm yields the following *aggregate demand for Old Masters*

$$L_t^d = \frac{\gamma \cdot W_t}{q_t - q_{t+1}/R_{t+1}} \stackrel{!}{=} L, \qquad (100)$$

which, in equilibrium, must equal the given supply, L. The reader may check this formula intuitively: With a Cobb-Douglas utility function, γ is known to equal the expenditure share of the corresponding good, while the denominator of (100) simply depicts the Old Master's shadow rent. For later purposes, we want first to rewrite (100) in the equivalent form

$$\frac{W_t}{q_t \cdot L - q_{t+1} \cdot L/R_{t+1}} = \frac{1}{\gamma}, \qquad (101)$$

and then solve it for the inverse of the interest factor:

$$\frac{1}{R_{t+1}} = \frac{q_t}{q_{t+1}} \cdot (1 - \frac{\gamma \cdot W_t}{q_t \cdot L}). \qquad (102)$$

Cancelling out the repeating terms q_t/q_{t+1} yields a simple expression for the corresponding compound interest factor:

$$\prod_{\tau=2}^{t} \frac{1}{R_\tau} = \frac{q_1}{q_t} \cdot \prod_{\tau=1}^{t-1} (1 - \frac{\gamma \cdot W_\tau}{q_\tau \cdot L}). \qquad (103)$$

The development of aggregate wage income is described by an exogenous sequence of *growth factors*, $G_t := W_t/W_{t-1}$. Thus compound growth $G_2 \cdot G_3 \cdot ... G_t$ is simply W_t/W_1. Combining this with (103) we obtain our final result:

$$\prod_{\tau=2}^{t} \frac{G_\tau}{R_\tau} = \frac{W_t}{q_t \cdot L} \cdot \frac{q_1 \cdot L}{W_1} \cdot \prod_{\tau=1}^{t-1} (1 - \frac{\gamma \cdot W_\tau}{q_\tau \cdot L}). \qquad (104)$$

From condition (77) we know that a growth path is dynamically efficient if the sequence (104) converges to zero as t approaches infinity. Now, the product (104) consists of two sequences and a constant real number $(q_1 \cdot L/W_1)$ in between. As q, L, R and γ are positive numbers, we readily infer by means of (101) that the left-hand sequence is bounded from above:

$$\frac{W_t}{q_t \cdot L} \leq \frac{W_t}{q_t \cdot L - q_{t+1} \cdot L/R_{t+1}} = \frac{1}{\gamma}, \qquad (105)$$

The right-hand sequence consists of factors which are all smaller than one and bounded away from one, too. This is because the total value of the Old Master, $q_\tau \cdot L$, may not exceed aggregate wage income, W_τ, which implies:

$$\frac{q_\tau \cdot L}{W_\tau} \leq 1 \quad \Leftrightarrow \quad \frac{W_\tau}{q_\tau \cdot L} \geq 1 \quad \Leftrightarrow \quad \frac{\gamma \cdot W_\tau}{q_\tau \cdot L} \geq \gamma > 0. \tag{106}$$

Now, as the left-hand sequence in (104) is bounded whilst the right-hand sequence converges to zero, the whole expression must also converge to zero, and any equilibrium is Pareto-efficient according to (77). It may well be that there is an infinity of equibria, or none at all, yet the households' optimization behaviour precludes the existence of equilibria which are dynamically inefficient.

In order to bring out the intuition behind this result, if necessary, we may consider an economy where aggregate income and the Old Master's price grow at the same constant rate. The increase in q_t yields a return to the holder of an Old Master which equals the growth rate. Since these goods are also a source of direct utility, the households will reject any offer to hold a useless asset whose interest *equals* the growth rate; therefore, interest on any useless asset must *exceed* the growth rate. But this is a sufficient condition for efficient economic growth. – The abstract analysis which has been conducted in chapter 4 demonstrates this reasoning to apply to fairly general economies; the only requirement being that the expenditure on Old Masters as a fraction of aggregate income does not vanish in the limit.

In concluding, let us add some remarks on the concept of *asset bubbles* in overlapping-generations models. These have been introduced by Tirole (1985) as a private means of overcoming dynamic inefficiency. A *bubble* is an asset which is completely useless and unproductive and on which reimbursements will never be made. One can think of a paper with the imprint: "I AM A BUBBLY ASSET". In the mentioned article, Tirole has shown that perfect foresight equilibria exist where the bubbly asset has a strictly positive price in every period. Using our own terminology, this is possible only if (i) the asset's price is non-negative in the first period (due to free disposal); (ii) if that price grows at least at the rate of interest (due to arbitrage); and (iii) if the total bubble, i.e. the total value of the bubbly asset, never exceeds aggregate income. Or formally, denoting the total bubble by b_t, the interest factor by R_t and aggregate income by Y_t, the existence of a bubble requires:

$$b_1 \geq 0, \tag{107}$$

$$b_t \geq R_t \cdot b_{t-1} \quad \text{for all } t \geq 2, \tag{108}$$

$$b_t \leq Y_t \quad \text{for all } t \geq 2. \tag{109}$$

These inequalities are identical to (73)-(75), our conditions for dynamic inefficiency. It is therefore immediate that bubbles can be ruled out precisely if dynamic inefficiency can be ruled out, by (77), for example. Since we have just shown (77) to apply in an economy with Old Masters, our above analysis already implies a non-existence result for bubbles. Bubbles can be found only in an economy without nonproducible durables, or on the condition that *all* these durables become perfectly irrelevant in far future.

However, we cannot distinguish empirically between bubbles and Old Masters unless we know the individual utility functions. Both types of commodities will roughly display the same price behaviour. But it occurs to me that pictures, stamps and the like are held at least partly because they yield direct utility – most often they are not considered to be a mere investment. Once this is true, the steady and often deplored rise in the price of such goods is quite understandable and cannot be interpreted as "speculation" – it is simply the consequence of the rise in aggregate income and the fact that Old Masters are not inferior. And then, people will refrain from setting up a bubble as the latter does not yield any direct utility.

6.6 A Simple Economy with an Exhaustible Resource

In chapter 5 we have argued that exhaustible resources – as opposed to land – will not prevent an economy from overaccumulating; moreover, these resources are *themselves* liable to being used inefficiently. This much is pretty plain, but it may be interesting to analyze the nature and causes of that inefficiency. In what follows we want to present a simple partial equilibrium model with an exhaustible resource, trace the development of the resource's stock over time, and discuss the problems of indeterminacy and inefficiency which will soon arise.

Our model consists of the following assumptions. At the inception of time, the economy is endowed with a given *stock*, S_1, of the resource which can be allocated arbitrarily over time, yet subject to the constraint $S_t \geq 0$ for all t. The *spot price* of the resource in period t is denoted by q_t in order to distinguish it from the forward prices used in chapter 5. The constant *interest factor*, given from outside, equals $R > 1$. In every period where $S_t > 0$, the resource's spot price grows at a rate which equals the interest rate, because otherwise the resource would either not be stored voluntarily or would yield a return exceeding the return on safe assets. This is the *Hotelling rule* which had been explained in depth in chapter 5 and which entails the following price behaviour:

$$\frac{q_t}{q_{t-1}} = R \quad \Rightarrow \quad q_t = q_1 \cdot R^{t-1}. \tag{110}$$

Finally, the *demand* for the resource at time t, denoted by D_t, is assumed to obey a constant iso-elastic relationship with the resource's spot price:

$$D_t = \frac{1}{q_t} \quad \Rightarrow \quad D_t = \frac{1}{q_1 \cdot R^{t-1}}, \tag{111}$$

where q_t has been substituted using (110). Thus, in every period the portion D_t of the total resource stock S_1 is used up (destroyed). Along a *feasible* path,

$$\sum_{t=1}^{\infty} D_t \leq S_1. \tag{112}$$

i.e. the total extraction of the resource may not exceed the initial stock. Since D_t is a geometric sequence, we can calculate the value of the associated geometric series as

$$\sum_{t=1}^{\infty} D_t = \frac{1/q_1}{1 - 1/R}. \tag{113}$$

The total demand for the exhaustible resource, aggregated over all periods, depends therefore on the given interest factor as well as on the endogenous price q_1. Combining (112) and (113) and solving for this initial price yields

$$q_1 \geq \frac{R}{r \cdot S_1}, \qquad (114)$$

where $r := R-1$ is the interest rate. Inequality (114), our final result, completely characterizes the set of perfect foresight equilibrium prices. Every q_1 meeting this condition entails that (i) buyers pick a quantity D_t according to their demand function, (ii) total demand does not exceed the total stock available, and (iii) the resource owners voluntarily keep the resource since they obtain a return which equals the interest rate.

Now, two problems immediately emerge. First, the equilibrium is obviously *indeterminate* because every q_1 satisfying (114) will do: In each period, the buyers pick a quantity according to their demand function, and the sellers are willing to supply exactly that quantity because they are indifferent between supplying and storing the resource (Hotelling rule). Thus every initial price fulfilling (114) constitutes a perfect foresight equilibrium which is feasible and in accordance with individual maximizing behaviour. Making allowance for the partial nature of the present model, the resulting state is, indeed, an equilibrium in the sense of definition (4).

Second, if the strict inequality holds in (114), the outcome is patently *inefficient* because, then, (110) will hold with strict inequality, too: The resource, though useful in every period, will not be used up even in the limit; the remaining stock S_t will be bounded away from zero. It would be a simple task for a planner (endowed with perfect foresight) to improve upon the resulting allocation by simply reducing q_1 to the level $R/(r \cdot S_1)$.

We have thus demonstrated how the competitive mechanism may fail to allocate exhaustible resources efficiently over time. But let us now try to point out the true cause of this seemingly strange occurence. Our explanation is at variance with substantial parts of the exhaustible resources literature. Dasgupta and Heal (1979; 163), for instance, after having outlined a quite similar example, formulated in continuous time, conclude:

6.6 A Simple Economy with an Exhaustible Resource

"[T]he foregoing example has brought out an important form of market failure. In the absence of a complete set of forward markets an indefinite sequence of momentary equilibria with fulfilled expectations could rather easily lead to an unpalatable outcome, one where the outcome results in too much conservation, not too little ... One way for the entire set of future possibilities to be taken into account at the initial date is for there to be a complete set of forward markets."

I do not believe the absense of a complete set of forward markets to be the genuine reason for the above inefficiency. As has been pointed out in section 2.5, the overlapping-generations model with perfect foresight may well be interpreted as an economy with a complete set of forward markets, its characteristic feature being that all agents have preferences for, and endowments of, only two neighbouring commodity bundles. Such does not violate the assumptions of the Arrow-Debreu model. The important deviation from that model is the existence of an unbounded horizon which entails the possibility of diverging series of commodity stocks. With a terminal date in our above example, inefficiency would never obtain since agents living in the last period would not store the resource but use it up completely.

Let us finally try to characterize the efficient use of a resource in terms of *interest and growth rates*. This is easy and at the same time completes our continuous aspiration to present a unifying theory of dynamic efficiency. We may first recall two things from the previous chapters. Let R_t denote a commodity's own rate of interest and G_t its own rate of growth (both expressed as factors). Then, dynamic efficiency prevails if the product $G_1/R_1 \cdot G_2/R_2...$ vanishes in the limit for all commodities. Moreover, the growth factors were applied to the total quantities, i.e. the *stocks*, in our efficiency formulae, not to the flows.

Now, a particular feature of an exhaustible resource is that its own rate of interest *vanishes* identically, which is the basic meaning of the Hotelling rule. Therefore, the resource's own rate of interest being *identically* equal to unity, the growth factors must be smaller than, and bounded away from, one; or equivalently, the resource's own rate of growth must be negative and bounded away from zero if dynamic efficiency is to be ensured. From (111), the remaining stock of the resource can be calculated using the familiar rules for finite geometric series:

$$S_{t+1} = S_1 - \sum_{\tau=1}^{t} D_\tau = S_1 - \frac{R^t - 1}{q_1 \cdot r \cdot R^{t-1}}. \tag{115}$$

The resources own rate of growth is thus

$$\frac{S_{t+1} - S_t}{S_t} = - \frac{r}{R + R^{t-1} \cdot (q_1 \cdot S_1 \cdot r - R)}. \tag{116}$$

We realized above that the resource will be completely used up if q_1 equals $R/(r \cdot S_1)$. In this case, the last expression becomes $-r/R$: the resource's own rate of growth is negative and bounded away from zero. As a consequence, the product $G_1/R_1 \cdot G_2/R_2...$ necessarily vanishes because the commodity own interest factors all equal unity, and the equilibrium is dynamically efficient. If, on the other hand, the initial price q_1 is "too high", the resource's own rate of growth will converge to zero, as can be seen directly from (116). Our sufficient critera for dynamic efficiency will then be violated.

This confirms again, and in a nice fashion, that exhaustible resources do not raise additional problems as far as dynamic efficiency is concerned. They, like all other commodities, must display own rates of interest which are greater than, and bounded away from, their own rates of growth if Pareto-optimality is to be ensured.

References

Aaron, H. (1966) The Social Insurance Paradox. *Canadian Journal of Economics and Political Science* **32**, pp. 371-374.

Abel, A.B., N.G. Mankiw, L.H. Summers and R.J. Zeckhauser (1989) Assessing Dynamic Efficiency: Theory and Evidence. *Review of Economic Studies* **56**, pp. 1-20.

Balasko, Y. and K. Shell (1980) The Overlapping-Generations Model, I: The Case of Pure Exchange without Money. *Journal of Economic Theory* **23**, pp. 281-306.

Balasko, Y., D. Cass and K. Shell (1980) Existence of Equilibrium in a General Overlapping-Generations Model. *Journal of Economic Theory* **23**, pp. 307-322.

Barro, R.J. (1974) Are Government Bonds Net Wealth? *Journal of Political Economy* **82**, pp. 1095-1117.

Boadway, R. (1989) The Short Run and Long Run Welfare Effects of Implementing a Practical System of Consumption Taxation. Unpublished paper, presented at a meeting in Heidelberg/FRG.

Böhm-Bawerk, E.v. (1913) Eine 'dynamische' Theorie des Kapitalzinses. *Zeitschrift für Volkswirtschaft, Sozialpolitik und Verwaltung* **22**, pp. 1-62 and 640-656.

Calvo, G.A. (1978) On the Indeterminacy of Interest Rates and Wages with Perfect Foresight. *Journal of Economic Theory* **19**, pp. 321-337.

Cass, D. (1972) On Capital Overaccumulation in the Aggregative, Neoclassical Model of Economic Growth: A Complete Characterization. *Journal of Economic Theory* **4**, pp. 200-223.

Cass, D. and M. Yaari (1966) A Re-Examination of the Pure Consumption Loans Model. *Journal of Political Economy* **74**, pp. 353-367.

Dasgupta, P. S. and G. M. Heal (1979) *Economic Theory and Exhaustible Resources*. Welwyn: James Nisbet & Co. Ltd.

Debreu, G. (1954) Valuation Equilibrium and Pareto Optimum. Reprinted in: Hildenbrand, W. (ed.) *Mathematical Economics: Twenty Papers of Gerard Debreu*. Cambridge etc.: Cambridge University Press.

Debreu, G. (1959) *Theory of Value*. New York: John Wiley & Sons.

Diamond, P. (1965) National Debt in a Neoclassical Growth Model. *American Economiy Review* **55**, pp. 1126-1150.

Eatwell J. (1987) Own Rates of Interest. In: *The New Palgrave. A Dictionary of Economics*. London and Basingstoke: Macmillan.

Faber, M. (1979) *Introduction to Modern Austrian Capital Theory*. Berlin etc.: Springer.

Feldstein, M.S. (1977a) The Surprising Incidence of a Tax on Pure Rent: A New Answer to an Old Question. *Journal of Political Economy* **85**, pp. 349-360.

Feldstein, M.S. (1977b) The Social Security Fund and National Capital Accumulation. In: *Funding Pensions: The Issues and Implications for Financial Markets*. Boston: Federal Reserve Bank.

Geanakoplos, J. (1987) Overlapping Generations Model of General Equilibrium. In: *The New Palgrave. A Dictionary of Economics*. London and Basingstoke: Macmillan.

Grandmont, J.-M. (1983) *Money and Value. A Reconsideration of Classical and Neoclassical Monetary Theories*. Cambridge etc.: Cambridge University Press.

Homburg, St. (1991) Interest and Growth in an Economy with Land. *Canadian Journal of Economics* **24**, pp.450-459.

Homer, S. (1963) *A History of Interest Rates*. New Brunswick etc.: Rutgers University Press.

Hoyt, H. (1933) *One Hundred Years of Land Values in Chicago*. Reprint Chicago 1970: The University of Chicago Press.

Kuenne, R.E. (1963) *The Theory of General Economic Equilibrium*. Princeton: Princeton University Press.

Lerner, A.P. (1959a) Consumption-Loan Interest and Money. *Journal of Political Economy* **67**, pp. 512-518 and Rejoinder, pp. 523-525.

Mackenroth, G. (1952) Die Reform der Sozialpolitik durch einen deutschen Sozialplan. In: *Schriften des Vereins für Socialpolitik*, N.F. **4**, Berlin: Duncker & Humblot.

Malinvaud, E. (1953) Capital Accumulation and Efficient Allocation of Resources. *Econometrica* **21**, pp. 233-268.

McCallum, B.T. (1987) The Optimal Inflation Rate in an Overlapping-Generations Economy with Land. In: W.A. Barnett and K.J. Singleton (eds.) *New Approaches to Monetary Economics*. Cambridge: Cambridge University Press.

McFadden, D., T. Mitra and M. Majumdar (1980) Pareto Optimality and Competitive Equilibrium in Infinite Horizon Economies. *Journal of Mathematical Economics* **7**, pp. 1-26.

Meinhold, H. (1985) Die ordnungspolitische Bedeutung des Versicherungsprinzips in der deutschen Sozialpolitik. In: Schmähl, W. (ed.) *Versicherungsprinzip und soziale Sicherung*. Tübingen: Mohr.

Merton, R.C. (1983) On the Role of Social Security in an Economy where Human Capital is not Tradable. In: Bodie, Z. and J.B. Shoven (ed.) *Financial Aspects of the United States Pension Scheme*. Chicago: The University of Chicago Press.

Muller, W.J. III and M. Woodford (1988) Determinacy of Equilibrium in Stationary Economies with Both Finite and Infinite Lived Consumers. *Journal of Economic Theory* **46**, pp. 255-290.

Niehans, J. (1966) Eine vernachlässigte Beziehung zwischen Bodenpreis, Wirtschaftswachstum und Kapitalzins. *Schweizerische Zeitschrift für Volkswirtschaft und Statistik* **102**, pp. 195-200.

Phelps, E. S. (1965) Second Essay on the Golden Rule of Accumulation. *American Economic Review* **55**, pp. 783-814.

Pigou, A.C. (1935) *The Economics of Stationary States*. London: Macmillan.

Rhee, C. (1991) Dynamic Inefficiency in an Economy with Land. *Review of Economic Studies* **58**, pp. 791-797.

Ricardo, D. (1817) *Principles of Political Economy and Taxation*. Reprint 1924 London: Bell and Sons.

Sachverständigenrat (1990) *Jahresgutachten 1990/91*. Bundestagsdrucksache 11/**8472**.

Samuelson, P.A. (1958) An Exact Consumption-Loan Model of Interest with or without the Social Contrivance of Money. *Journal of Political Economy* **66**, pp. 467-482.

Scheinkman, J.A. (1980) Notes on Asset Tradin in an Overlapping Generations Model. University of Chicago, mimeo.

Schumpeter, J.A. (1913) Eine 'dynamische' Theorie des Kapitalzinses – Eine Entgegnung. *Zeitschrift für Volkswirtschaft, Sozialpolitik und Verwaltung* **22**, pp. 699-639.

Shell, K. (1971) Notes on the Economics of Infinity. *Journal of Political Economy* **79**, pp. 1002-1011.

Spremann, K. (1984) Intergenerational Contracts and Their Decomposition. *Journal of Economics* **44**, pp. 237-253.

Starrett, D. (1970) The Efficiency of Competitive Programs. *Econometrica* **38**, pp. 704-711.

Stephan, G. and G. Wagenhals (1990) Innovation, Decentralization and Equilibrium. *Schweizerische Zeitschrift für Volkswirtschaft und Statistik* **126**, pp. 129-145.

Tirole, J. (1985) Asset Bubbles and Overlapping Generations. *Econometrica* **53**, pp. 1071-1100.

Tobin, J. (1980) Discussion. In: Kareken, J.H and N. Wallace (ed.) *Models of Monetary Economics*. Minneapolis: Federal Reserve Bank of Minneapolis.

Turgot, A.R.J. (1766) *Réflexion sur la formation et la distribution des richesses*. Paris: Par. M.Y.

Weil, P. (1987) Love Thy Children. Reflections on the Barro Debt Neutrality Theorem. *Journal of Monetary Economics* **19**, pp. 377-391.

Wicksell, K. (1934) *Lectures on Political Economy*. London: Routledge and Kegen Paul.

Wright, R.(1987) Market Structure and Competitive Equilibrium in Dynamic Economic Models. *Journal of Economic Theory* **41**, pp.189-201.

Name Index

Aaron, H. 85
Abel, A.B. 34, 36

Balasko, Y. 2, 13, 19, 21, 30, 66, 67
Barro, R.J. 1
Boadway, R. 66
Böhm-Bawerk, E.v. 78, 80, 81

Calvo, G.A. 39, 89
Cass, D. 2, 6, 19, 21, 25, 50, 66

Dasgupta, P.S. 61, 63, 94
Debreu, G. 5, 9, 14, 19
Diamond, P. 19, 23, 37, 70, 71, 73, 74, 75, 77, 81

Eatwell, J. 26

Faber, M. 80
Feldstein, M.S. 39, 83

Geanakoplos, J. 23
Grandmont, J.-M. 14

Heal, G.M. 61, 63, 94
Homburg, St. 72
Homer, S. 78
Hoyt, H. 76

Keynes, J.-M. 26, 81
Knight, F. 81
Kuenne, R.E. 80

Lerner, A.P. 83
Louis XVI. 78

Mackenroth, G. 83
Majumdar, M. 12, 19
Malinvaud, E. 6, 12, 25, 81
Mankiw, N.G. 34
McCallum, B. T. 39, 72
McFadden, D. 12, 19
Meinhold, H. 83
Merton, R.C. 87
Mitra, T. 12, 19
Muller, W.J. III 81

Niehans, J. 81

Phelps, E.S. 66
Pigou, A.C. 80f.

Quesnay, F. 78

Rhee, C. 39, 76
Ricardo, D. 82, 88

Samuelson, P.A. 12, 19, 25, 66, 77, 81, 82, 85
Scheinkman, J.A. 39
Schönfelder, B. 72
Schumpeter, J.A. 80, 81
Shell, K. 2, 13, 19, 20, 21, 30, 66, 67
Spremann, K. 67
Starrett, D. 25

Stephan, G. 12
Summers, L.H. 34

Tirole, J. 81, 91
Tobin, J. 86
Turgot, A.R.J. 78ff.

Wagenhals, G. 12

Weil, P. 1
Wicksell, K. 80, 81
Woodford, M. 81
Wright, R. 20

Yaari, M. 19

Zeckhauser, R.J. 34

Subject Index

Aggregate expenditure 18
Aggregate profits 18
Aggregate wealth 21
Allocations **6f.**
Arrow-Debreu model 1, 3, 95
Assets 14, **26**
Asset-augmented economy **28**
Average interest rate 33

Bar, use of **7**
Bequest motive 2
Bonds 14
Bubbles 88, 91, 92

Capital productivity 82
Capital reserve system 83ff.
Cash Flow **8**, 35
Cash Flow Criterion 34, 36
Cobb-Douglas function 39, 72, 75, 84, 90
Commodities **4**
Commodity bundles **5**
Competitive equilibrium **7**
Compound interest rate 33
Consumption sets 4

Denier du prix du terres 78ff.
Determinacy of equilibrium 3
Double infinity 19
Durable goods 14
Dynamic efficiency **1**, 9, 15
– and cash flow 35
– and exhaustible resources 59

– and fiscal policy 50
– and land 39, 47
– and generational transfers 71
– in a macromodel 65ff.
– in a stationary state 79
– interpretation of 23

Dynamic production 5, 6

Efficiency of equilibrium 3
Endowments **4, 13**
Exchange Economy 13
Exhaustible resources **54**
– demand for 93
– efficient use of 63, 64, 95
– in a macromodel 92ff.
Existence of equilibrium 3

Financial illusion 83
Firms 4, 5
Forward prices 30

Golden rule of accumulation 75
Government bonds 70

Hotelling rule 57ff., 63, 93ff.
Households 4
Household's consumption **5**

Implicit rate of return 85
Indeterminacy of equilibrium 89, 94
Interest and Growth 31
Interest factor 68, 73, 27, 25

Subject Index

Land **40**
– and generational transfers 86
– as a demand for housing 88
– in a macromodel 71ff.
– price of 76
– rental market for 45
– stock market for 45

Land's income share **46,** 75, 76
Land/labour ratio 74
Laspeyres index 31, 33
Leisure 5
Limit infimum 70

Market value of firms 35
Money 14

National income **9,** 16, 31, 68
Nominal interest factor **32**
Notational conventions 3

Old Masters 88ff.
Optimal economic growth 1
Overaccumulation 35, 66, 77
Own rates of growth **25**
Own rates of interest **25**

Paasche index 32, 33
Pareto-improving transfers 69f.
Pareto-optimum 1, **7,** 9, 13, 17, 20, 32, 47, 49, 61, 75, 91
Pay-as-you-go system 83
Perishable goods 14, 17, 26
Population and social security 83
Population growth 74

Population growth rate 84
Preference ordering 4
Present value 4
Prices 4
Productive exhaustible resource 57
Productive land **43**

Real growth factor **31,** 68, 90
Real interest factor **32,** 90, 93
Rent from land **45**
Returns to scale 35

Series of rents 48
Shadow rent 89
Social contract 77, 81, 86
Spot price 30, 65
– of a resource 93
Static production 5, 6
Stationary state 78
Steady state growth factor 75
Steady state interest factor 75
Stochastic dominance 87
Storable goods 14, **15,** 26

Theory of fructification 78ff.
Time preference 82
Transfer scheme **68**
Transfers between generations 86
Truncated economy 23

Useful exhaustible resource 55
Useful land **42**
Utility function 68

Valuation equilibrium 19

Printing: Druckhaus Beltz, Hemsbach
Binding: Buchbinderei Schäffer, Grünstadt